Bio-One:

MAVERICK FRANCHISE

How a tight budget, a desire to help, and a hunger for success can become your greatest competitive advantage

Nick-Anthony Zamucen
Copyright © 2016 Bio-One, INC

Published in the United States by Bio-One, INC.

Zamucen, Nick-Anthony, author.

Bio-One MAVERICK FRANCHISE: How a tight budget, a desire to help, and a hunger for success can become your greatest competitive advantage/ Nick-Anthony Zamucen.

– First edition.

1. New business enterprises.

2. Franchising.

3. Success in business.

4. Creative ability in franchising.

5. Strategic planning.

6. Entrepreneurship.

ISBN-13: 978-1534901919
ISBN-10: 1534901914

Dedication

This book is dedicated to my son, Gavin Michael Zamucen. "Bio-One Inc" wouldn't have been created if it wasn't for you. Thank you for being my inspiration, dive and force of focus in this crazy world. Hard Work Pays Off! Always remember I love you, your sister Cali Grace and of course your beautiful mother and angel in my corner, my love, my wife, my life, Molly.

Bio-One:
MAVERICK FRANCHISE
How a tight budget, a desire to help, and a hunger for success
can become your greatest competitive advantage

Table of Contents

**❝❝I believe life is constantly testing us for our level
of commitment, and life's greatest rewards
are reserved for those who demonstrate a
never-ending commitment to act until they
achieve. This level of resolve can move mountains,
but it must be constant and consistent. Your past
does not equal your future and you must live
in an attitude of gratitude, because life is
happening for you, not to you.❞❞**

– Anthony Robbins

Introduction

"Our greatest weakness lies in giving up. The most certain way to succeed is always to try just one more time." – Thomas Edison

If you give up and walk away from your dreams now, then failure is most definitely the direct result. However, if you keep trying and continue to take action, you will succeed. Maybe not in the way you intended, but you will succeed nonetheless.

Over twenty years ago, I took the step to transition from the world of Corporate America and pursue a dream of developing my own business after attending church where my minister had told the congregation of a horrible incident that occurred where the husband of one of the church members had sorrowfully committed suicide. The wife had not attended church and the minister knew that she needed to be comforted, and I took the opportunity to volunteer to help provide some level of assistance during this troubling time for the fellow church member and her family. I joined the minister with several other individuals and went to meet the wife at the house where her husband had taken his own life. After the police had told her that she would be forced to clean the area affected by what occurred, the wife had become even more traumatized by what had occurred and could not gain enough energy to move from her couch for several days.

Seeing an immediate need to help another individual during a time that caused her much great stress and emotional trauma, I jumped into cleaning the house while several others took the wife out to lunch to help calm her nerves. At this moment, I saw that a core belief that needed to be established with similar situations is that of helping individuals first, then doing the business second. After seeing this one traumatic event that was faced by a fellow church member, I knew that there were probably people from around the country that faced similar situations every day and the idea for Bio-One was born.

The idea that sparked into a small business approximately twenty years ago has transitioned into a franchise-based company, Bio-One Inc, where we now help to serve individuals, families and businesses in over 36 states, and continue growing at an exceptional rate, reflecting a 100% Success Rate for franchise ownership. My goal, as a business owner and leader, has always been to help share success and to create an informative and educational franchise that breeds success continually. It is my goal that, through this book, you will be able to find your personal journey of success through investing in a franchise. I will help provide a full range of topics and recommendations that will help you to succeed in any franchise decision, not only Bio-One. From determining what is the best franchise for you to being able to better-market your new investment, I will provide some of the valuable knowledge and insight that I have gained through my experiences and help to share in the ideals of success.

Current Trends in Franchising and Why Now?

In 2016, the total number of franchises within the United States totals over 795,000 and are anticipated to maintain fortifiable growth over the coming year. With a forecast of 1.7 percent growth in 2016, despite some worries of economic downturn, solid growth is to be expected. The continued growth in the franchise industry is accompanied by a maintained acceleration in business spending and a continued momentum shift after 2015 saw a stronger-than-expected growth, according to the 2016 Franchise Business Economic Outlook, published by HIS Economics. As compared to other industries of commerce, franchises will continue to grow at exceptional rates in comparison, with several key factors being attributable alongside an increase in employment and Gross Domestic Product.

In addition to forecast models illustrating improvement in franchise performance, employment forecasts are set to increase by over 3 percent, or 9 Million Franchise jobs, in 2016 and a total of $552 Billion generated Gross Domestic Product (GDP), increasing from $523 Billion GDP in the previous year of 2015. This continued growth in the franchise industry has been maintained since 2010, being recognized as a consistent growth-industry over a 5 year spectrum.

The enhanced benefits and attributable gains realized by hundreds of thousands of franchises throughout the United States and throughout the world make the industry a lightning rod to many entrepreneurs that look to take part in the success and high amount of energy that is demonstrated by the industry. With a positive element being demonstrated by the franchise industry for so many years, many individuals lose sight of the diligence and thought process that takes place in order to develop the level of success that has been realized. To help ensure that those with an entrepreneurial dream find fulfillment, throughout this book, we will take a closer look at the success story of a franchise, Bio-One, and a full range of considerations to take into account as an aspiring franchisee to develop a foundation for triumph.

With over $550 Billion being distributed through the Gross Domestic Product of the franchise industry, time is of the essence for many to create meaningful success within a relatively short amount of time. As an individual that has already decided to take a closer look at this book, now is also a critical time to take opportunity of a new challenge and potential for success in your life that will continually inspire you and help to provide experiences that will make you a better leader. By having the desire to succeed, you demonstrate the need to get started sooner, rather than later, with becoming a franchisee.

In the following sections, we will review information ranging from finding the right franchise to invest in to how to effectively market a new franchise. With key elements and tips from leading industry experts and role models, as well as the experience that I have developed as the founder and Chief Executive Officer of the Bio-One Franchise, this book has been specifically designed for you in mind and will help you to reach the goals that you have been dreaming long and hard about in becoming a successful franchisee.

Finding the Right Franchise

"A creative man is motivated by the desire to achieve, not by the desire to beat others."

– Ayn Rand

When it comes to business success, your goal will more likely be achieved when it deals with bettering yourself, not beating out others. Remember this as you decide why it is you want to own your own franchise or small business to begin with.

Throughout each of the next sections in this book, we will be guided into several methods that I hope to help you find the right franchise for you and help to provide a foundation of knowledge to help realize the success that you are working to achieve. It is my hope that you are able to find success and are able to pursue an opportunity that fits within your passions; if this opportunity comes with pursuing a franchise with Bio-One, I will be here to welcome you first hand, and if you decide that other franchise opportunities may be the right fit for you, I will also be here to be the first to say congratulations and know that you will be successful when this passion for accomplishment is found.

When I first started out when looking for something new and different beyond the norm that I had created in my personal life and career, I was not sure where life was going to take me, and it is with this example in mind that I would like to first share more of my personal story and the story of how Bio-One became into being before analyzing additional methods and information available in finding the right franchise for you.

Thank you for taking the first steps in this journey and, sincerely, best of luck in finding the right franchise for you.

Expect problems and eat them for breakfast.
– Alfred Montapert

The more you can anticipate the challenges you will face, the better you will be prepared when they arrive. Plan to take them on with the strength of a small army and you will conquer them in the end.

How the Business Idea was Born- History of Bio-One

As discussed in the introduction, the beginning of Bio-One started about twenty years ago after a fellow church member came in a time of need after her husband had sadly taken his own life. After the local police had finished their inspection and logistics, they left the wife with the traumatizing aftermath from the suicide that had occurred. Now, rather than just being a victim once, having to cope with the loss of her husband, the woman had to face another traumatic situation thinking about how to clean and start over again, if that were even conceivable. With the mindset of trying to help an individual in need, I took the time to go to the home with the church minister and found myself helping to clean the house while several others took the wife to a local restaurant to try and help her begin the process and long road of healing that would be faced.

After helping the church member in getting through this traumatic situation, I took a step back and realized that similar situations are unfortunately faced by countless individuals throughout the country and throughout the world every day and require someone that is able to assist in the process without being traumatized further. With the simple idea of helping others in mind, the beginning of Bio-One started that day. Out of great tragedy, comes great opportunity.

From the very first client over twenty years ago to now, we have helped meet the needs of individuals, families and businesses in 36 states throughout the United States and are planning on launching Bio-One Inc International soon, to expand our services even further. Every step along the way, I have never lost sight of the fundamental, "Help first, business second." This is something that you will hear me repeat several times as the incorporation to this ideal is at the foundation of Bio-One and the leadership that I portray with any organization I am a part of. I feel that it is critical to always help others and provide a service that is based in quality and ethical wellbeing and it is in that that I am excited to be able to share the journey and opportunity of owning a franchise with all those interested, including you through this book.

Overview of Bio-One Services

"Without hard work, nothing grows but weeds"
– Gordon Hinckley

In order to expect your new business to be a success, prepare to work. You can't just throw a bunch of seeds out into the wind and expect a high yield crop. You have to be willing to put in effort from sun up to sun down to get where you want to go.

Being referred to as the "last responders" we at Bio-One consistently work to provide outstanding and personable service to clients that have become victims of various situations that require emergency cleanup. At Bio-One, the work clock does not end at 5 PM or close down for the weekends- tragedies and events that require our highly effective services occur 24 hours a day, 7 days a week, and require us to be able to be available when needed by the communities in which we serve. In each of the services performed, we add value and a personal relationship with clients, always ensuring to never re-victimize an individual that has already faced tremendous stress or emotional turmoil. Let's take a closer look at some of the most common services performed at Bio-One with communities across the United States, and now spanning internationally.

Suicide, Homicide, and Decomposition Cleanup

After the police and investigators leave a home or business that a suicide or homicide has occurred, families, friends and co-workers are forced to take the first step in putting their lives back together after the loss experienced- cleaning up and working to reestablish the "norm" or status quo. After the police and coroner leaves the scene, Bio-One steps in to help begin to sanitize the area that was impacted by the event and also make a recovery of the emotional standing of individuals that have become victimized throughout the process. We go beyond cleaning a home or business, and we work to mend the hearts of those impacted with great tragedy, always keeping in mind that we are helping people, not just the business we operate.

In addition to active-based crimes or events, Bio-One is also recognized for the ability to come into cleanup situations that have faced decomposition or undiscovered deaths. There are unfortunate situations where individuals may pass away in their homes and go several days or weeks before being noticed by neighbors, friends, or family, and there is an additional sense of need developed to have a professional and qualified organization provide cleanup for the situation that has occurred. Bio-One possesses the equipment and skill set necessary to meet the need in these situations and do so in a professional manner that makes the client feel comfortable and peaceful in knowing that a company that keeps their interests and welfare in mind is conducting the service.

Blood Spill Cleanup

Not all emergencies and personal disasters end with the police being involved, but the need to clean the mess left behind will remain. At Bio-One, we step in to quickly and safely clean blood and other blood-borne pathogens that carry disease and could become highly dangerous if left unattended without our assistance.

Hoarding Cleanup

There have been entire television shows dedicated to following stories of hoarding and they each depict the incredible illustration of what the interior of a house can look like after years of the hoarding activity is conducted. Many times, families are left with the question and uncertainty of what to do when someone in their own family-unit has become a personal victim of the disease of hoarding. Hoarding, itself, can create tremendous health hazards and safety concerns in addition to physical strain in the cleanup process. Bio-One has been established and recognized as a method to help get homes and lives back on track for families that have become victims of hoarding. Ranging from calls from realtors looking to market a property to a family member needing a hoarding-intervention, Bio-One will be there to assist and get lives back to normal after hoarding situations take place.

Medical Waste Disposal

Based on a National Health Expenditure Projection conducted by the Center for Medical Services in the United States, the spending on healthcare and related expenditures is expected to grow at an average rate of 5.8 percent through the year 2022. With increased spending in healthcare and additional needs identified for an aging population of Baby Boomers, the need for medical waste disposal is an increasing need that will only continue to develop in the United States and globally within the next decade. At Bio-One, services are conducted for individuals and businesses to help transport and dispose any biohazard or medical waste that must be separated from traditional waste materials. The special handling of biohazard and medical waste is critical to the safety of communities and presents a high need for the services that Bio-One performs. By providing peace of mind through expertise and positive actions in helping to make communities a safer place through biohazard and medical cleanup, Bio-One works to create lasting positive impressions in the communities in which we serve. We take care of the dangerous cleanups so others can be safe.

Emergency Vehicle Decontamination

When was the last time that you thanked a first responder or emergency responder, such as an EMT, police officer, or firefighter for what they do on a daily basis? These first responders risk their lives almost every day, putting themselves in challenging and dangerous situations to aid the communities in which they are involved.

Throughout the course of the actions that first responders and emergency personnel undergo on a daily basis, there often comes a time where the need for an emergency cleanup of greater proportions in comparison to what they are normally suited to provide solutions is required. Bio-One, as the "last responder" works hand-in-hand with the first responders throughout the United States, and internationally, to provide emergency vehicle decontamination and sanitation.

Later, we will discuss community relationships that help to benefit the franchise model of Bio-One and this is one key element that will come up again. By providing a tremendous service for the community first responders and emergency personnel, Bio-One works to create cross-communicational relationships and networking that will yield additional results into the future.

Odor Removal

There are truly thousands of reasons why odors occur in a home or business, both on a short term and long term standpoint. Bio-One, in addition to physical decomposition, blood, and additional cleanup needs, is able to use specialized equipment to help cancel and eliminate odors found in the home or business in question. By providing effective and proactive service in a timely manner, Bio-One can help individuals leave more peacefully within their homes or can help a business to be more profitable by ensuring that clients are not turned away for a given situation that may have occurred.

Teargas Cleanup

Whether it is due to anti-riot actions, or tactical entry, or accidental utilization, Bio-One is able to clean the residue left behind from teargas deployment. The somewhat sticky substance created by teargas can cause issues by leaving residue on items it touches if they are not quickly and efficiently cleaned off. This is where Bio-One comes in, to help serve the communities and individuals that become victims of teargas deployment, and do so within a timely manner.

Mold Remediation

After Hurricane Katrina devastated thousands of homes and businesses along the Gulf Coast in 2005, the after-effects of cleanup were perhaps more daunting than the initial cleanup of debris and water movement. The massive amount of water that came pouring into the southerly region of the United States caused an incredible amount of sustained and worrisome damage through mold growth. Mold is identified as a substance that can cause incredible health concerns through airborne pathogens. The factors of mold can be especially harmful for young children or elderly individuals within a household with easily-compromised immune systems, but are a bothersome issue for most all families in the United States, especially in areas susceptible to flooding or high humidity levels where mold thrives.

To help alleviate health concerns surrounding mold growth and to provide communities with a direct means of clean up when these situations occur, Bio-One is yet again ready to be called upon to fill the need.

Feces, Urine and Droppings Cleanup

Right on top of the list with things that you never want to see in a home or business, alongside mold, is most likely that of coming across feces, urine or rodent droppings that require immediate attention to be cleaned. Being identified as being highly dangerous, fecal matter that has been left behind by both humans and animals should be immediately and properly cleaned by an established service organization.

The process of rodent cleanup can stretch beyond that of feces and urine and can actually include helping to finish the job when it comes to rodents and working to create a plan for specific clients to be rid of rodents for the long term. Rather than a "one and done" process, Bio-One is committed to providing lasting results for the communities in which we provide top quality services.

Sewage Backups

From pipes collapsing and clogging to construction taking place along city streets, there are a multitude of reasons where plumbing may be impacted and can cause a significant need to have a sewage backup situation take hold of a home or business. When these situations occur, Bio-One steps into action and works to eliminate or minimize potential diseases that would become prevalent if the cleanup situation went unmonitored or actionable.

At Bio-One, we always look for the next opportunity to put people first and business second and this is shown in each level of job that we pursue and complete for clients around the world. By being constantly prepared to provide solutions to unanticipated events, Bio-One continues to develop much needed trust within the community that we serve, helping to create lifelong business channels. In addition to the example listed above, Bio-One participates in additional cleanup and business continuation services that are not listed and should be considered before diving headfirst into the franchise option.

A Story of Success- Nick-Anthony Zamucen

❝*Optimism is the faith that leads to achievement. Nothing can be done without hope and confidence.*❞ – Helen Keller

Be positive, have faith that you're on the right path, and never lose hope that great things lie ahead. These three virtues will take you further toward your business success than most any other virtues that exist.

Holding the title of founder and Chief Executive Officer at Bio-One, or for any organization for that matter, is something that once upon a time I had actually never considered. Before Bio-One, I was sitting in the corporate world, partially content with the fact that my career would be guided by others, at the hand of not my own. But one day that mindset changed and I was in pursuit of something that could become greater, not only for myself and my family, but in the community I am a part of, both locally and beyond. I knew that I had more to offer as a leader and was willing to start making a conscious decision to find an opportunity that I could pursue that broke away from the mold that I had known for so long.

As you are reading this book, you may be envisioning yourself in a new situation- something different than the past norm that you have become accustomed to within a corporation or business model that essentially creates the mold for which you will follow, but you are finding yourself with the thought that you want something different. You want to be successful and you want to be able to control the ability to attain the goals that you have thought long and hard about, pondering and wondering of how life can be better and how you can achieve a given level that you see so many others achieving around you. This is where my story meets yours-the opportunity for success at hand and starting to focus on that mindset in which you want to inspire a change in your life to be the one in charge, no one else, but you. To succeed in life, in business, in family, and in any realm where success is possible, you must first maintain the mindset that you can achieve success, and all actions will follow- Success Breeds Success.

Throughout my life, religion has been an important foundation that I have held and has helped to guide the leadership models and actions that I follow, continually working to lead with a high degree of ethics and mutual respect for all that I work with. It was when I was attending church in Georgia, nearly two decades ago, where the idea for Bio-One was born. In my mind, I had the vision for something different in my life and knew that it was possible to succeed beyond where I was currently, and it was with this mindset that I took to heart a situation that presented itself that became of light from the words of the Pastor at that church in Georgia.

The day where my life forever changed as a part of Bio-One was when the Pastor said that a man had taken his own life and asked if individuals at the church would help pay a visit to his wife. When myself and a few others went to meet the shaken woman, we found her with a home that had become a tragic scene by the events of her husband taking his own life, with the police and emergency responders leaving the scene to be cleaned by her. In my mind, I knew immediately that I needed to help jump into action and my heart poured out for this woman standing before me that had not only become a victim by the tragic situation of her husband taking her own life, but she had also become a victim once again when police officers and first responders said that they could not assist her with helping to bring her life back into order. It was there, in that small town in Georgia that the idea for Bio-One and helping others through tragic and complicated situations that required cleanup and restoration became possible.

Taking into account the vision I have always maintained, helping people first and then looking toward the business, became into swift action with Bio-One just over 19 years ago and as of today, we are running at over 40 franchise locations throughout the United States and looking toward additional expansion, including internationally. From the beginning, I knew that the business model was going to be successful if I was willing to put in the work necessary to make it successful and knowing that if I were to help others find similar success and focus in their lives, the idea of people helping people through business could become even more so realized. As the Chief Executive Officer of Bio-One, I have made it a priority to help inspire success in others and make it possible for additional franchisees to succeed. By investing in training with each franchisee and providing personal support and guidance, I work to create a better business each day and also work to help make others more successful through their abilities and actions at Bio-One.

I understood from an early point that it takes hard work to succeed and that maintaining a high level of ethics is incredibly important in creating sustainability, and it is with both elements in mind that I continue to focus on the success of each individual within Bio-One and the organization as a whole. It is with this vision that I additionally look forward to continuing to assist others, such as you, into the future for being able to realize their full potential and attain the next level of success that they wish to fulfill.

Testimonial 1: Matt Mistica, Bio-One

❝What you get by achieving your goals is not as important as what you become by achieving your goals.❞ – Henry David Thoreau

Don't wait to the end of your new business venture to celebrate your successes. Enjoy the journey along the way and be proud of what you are accomplishing as this will keep you moving in the right direction.

As part of my goal with this book in helping to provide a "Guide to Franchising," I wanted to give you, as a reader, an insight into the first hand success that several of the franchisees at Bio-One have attributed. In this first testimonial, you will have the opportunity to gain a perspective from one of our newest franchisees, Matt Mistica, based in Houston and Austin, Texas. To help provide an unbiased perspective to potential franchisees searching for the right fit, the interviews were conducted with a third-party and then added to the book. Take a look at the interview snapshot conducted with Matt Mistica as a valuable member of the Bio-One Team.

Q: Where are you Located?

A: Located in Houston and Austin with Bio-One. I have been involved with Bio-One for about 2 years.

Q: Would you consider yourself an entrepreneur and business owner in the past, before Bio-One?

A: Bio-One is my first "real" business. When I was in college, I had some small tutoring business and things, but nothing as full time and involved as Bio-One. Before starting the Bio-One franchise, I was working in the corporate space in the oil and gas industry.

Q: Why franchising and why Bio-One?

A: It is an unconventional business model, but I feel that I am someone that thinks outside of the box and Bio-One fit right into that description. I think that in order for you to be a successful business person, you must leverage what you are good at and a little bit of business savvy with your passions. At Bio-One we believe in Helping First, Business Second. I feel that I am a compassionate person and Bio-One helped leverage that skill set to grow and be a successful business.

Q: How did you find out about Bio-One and did you consider other business models before choosing this franchise?

A: I was looking at a myriad of business, including traditional business models that provided products and services such as making and selling sandwiches or ice cream, or real-estate related companies and other traditional-type cleaning companies. After about 4 months of research, I came across Bio-One and once I looked into the company and did my due diligence and reached out to individuals within the organization, I was immediately hooked. Here we are 2 years later.

Q: What does it take to be successful in the franchising industry?

A: Just because you have a franchise does not mean that success will automatically follow suit, however it is a good starting point. A good thing about having a franchise is that there is a base foundation that you can grow off of and there is a business model that has been tried and true. But just because someone else has been successful with a franchise, from Bio-One to McDonalds, does not necessarily mean that you are going to be successful. You have to work hard, get the name out there, and let people know that you are in business and able to help add value to prospective clients.

Q: What are the 4 mistakes that people make when looking for a franchise?

1. If you are looking for the wrong reasons- if you are looking to choose a franchise because you just do not like your job and willing to do anything, this would be a mistake. You need to be passionate about what you do and what you are going into

as a franchise, you don't want to chose a franchise just to get away from your current employment or career.

2. Don't go into a franchise just because someone that you know that went into the same franchise was successful, such as your family or friends. Just because someone else was successful within the franchise and business model, does not necessarily mean that it will be a good fit for you.

3. Not doing enough, or an adequate amount, of research before pursuing the franchise. If you come across a franchise and like the logo and website and decide that you want to jump into it, there is a lot more that needs to be considered and that should be taken into account because there is a lot more to a franchise than what meets the eye. You need to have your due diligence and hope that the choice you make is the right one.

4. Approval seeking- If you are making a change, whether it be a career move or business move or if there is a major life change, there will be a large amount of individuals that may criticize your decision, and there will always be some that either support the decision being made or think that it is not a good idea for you. It is always good to get input from others, but at the end of the day, ask yourself the question, "Who is going to be the one that is buying into the franchise? Is it going to be me or my friends, or those who criticize or provide feedback, that are going to be the ones making the investment in Bio-One or the given franchise?" Realizing that it is "Me" is important. Don't let anyone sway your decision to either move forward or back away because it is, in the end, your decision to make the investment, in yourself and your family.

Q: What is the best personality type that will succeed in the franchise industry?

A: No matter what, with franchising and having a business, ambition is number 1. It is good to be intelligent; it is good to be a people person; it is good to be business savvy, but if you are not going to get up off the couch and you don't have a dream or a vision as to what you are going to do with this model, then you are not going to go anywhere with the franchise. The number one attribute that I feel has served me well and other entrepreneurs and franchisees is being ambitious and having the "Never Say Die" type attitude.

Q: How did you let people in your community know that you exist as a franchise/business and how did you find clients? What was your best marketing technique?

A: I was, and still am, very excited about my business and feel that my clients, both past, present and future and prospective clients can feed off of that excitement. I am excited about my business and feel that we provide a really great service that can add value to organizations- whether it be a corporation, law enforcement, home owners association, board of directors for other businesses and commercial businesses, you name it! It is a value proposition where I feel that I can add value to others and that enthusiasm is something that has resonated with a lot of people and truly works in any arena. Enthusiasm for my company spills over with all areas-department communities from local law enforcement- letting them know that we are a resource and better than alternatives in the market.

Q: When did you feel that your franchise with Bio-One was "Going to make it?"

A: We did break-even within the first year and that is a big milestone that any business wants to achieve. By being able to reach this milestone within the first year identifies that you are involved with a good business. After achieving that first milestone, I was very happy in that I knew we worked hard to achieve the goals set.

Q: How many people do you have on your team?

A: At the moment, we have 3 employees plus me, for a total of 4 team members. If we have to contract labor we do, but most of the time we can handle any situation with 2 team members and a truck.

Q: Where do you see Bio-One in the Houston and Austin regions in the next 5 years?

A: We are slowly continuing to grab market share every day and I envision that within that timeframe, when a situation where in Houston and Austin, it doesn't become a question of individuals asking, "Which business are we going to contact to get a situation handled, or this or that cleaned up, or this remediated?" I don't want it to be a question- I want it to be a top of mind response that when any related situations come into existence, Bio-One Houston or Bio-One Austin are automatically top-of-mind. We want to keep thought within Bio-One.

So far, we have been growing in leaps and bounds in the past two years and I am happy as to where things have progressed and look forward to the movement of business more and more toward the five year goal that I have in mind.

Q: How long did it take for the transition between day one of franchising to launch?

A: It took approximately 2 and half months to launch. Having a conversation with Nick is where it all started- Nick is a great guy that is identified as being a wealth of knowledge with Bio-One and how to run and be a successful business owner. Additionally, Nick is one that provides experiences that allow me to emulate him as a leader and individual, both in a business setting and in my personal life. Nick is probably the main reason as to why I chose to go with Bio-One as he continually stresses the importance of having family dynamics within the business model, from an individual franchise-level, to the organization as a whole.

Q: How old were you when you first started the Bio-One Franchise?

A: I am able to attest that Bio-One is compatible to fulfill the dreams of a full range of franchisees as I started at the age of 28 with a Bio-One franchisee.

Q: Is there anything else that you can add for those interested in getting into the business of starting a franchise?

A: I like the franchising model because it is not an unchartered territory. A franchise is a proven business model that works and that was something that intrigued me with Bio-One and seeing the success that Nick has developed with the organization, as long as with being a kind and caring person. In addition, being able to lean on the experience of other new franchisees within Bio-One was a part of the family dynamics of the organization that helped to make things less stressful in comparison to running a business truly "on your own."

Having a foundation and family dynamic within Bio-One is something to be considered if someone is interested in joining into the franchise industry.

Q: What is the best way to get in touch with you?

A: I am Matt Mistica at Bio-One Houston and can be reached directly at 832-444-8352

"I am a regular guy trying to make my way in this world."

-Matt Mistica

Bio-One Houston & Bio-One Austin

Quality Franchisor

Think, for a moment, about what is most important for you when it comes to choosing from an array of options in business. When you are going to make a decision for purchase, whether it be for a specific product or service, is one of the first things that comes to mind how you are treated as an individual? Or, let's put it another way- If a business came to you and said that they were willing to get to know you as a person and meet the needs that you are seeking before ever asking for any payment or compensation in return, how would that make you feel? That feeling that you are thinking about right now is one that you want to be able to carry forward in the investment of a franchise that you are thinking about. So, whether you are thinking about pursuing a franchise with Bio-One or the thousands of other available options available for a franchise around the globe, think to yourself, are you going to be able to put people first and business second?

"Help First, Business Second."

This simple phrase, "Help First, Business Second," is one that you will often hear from me and the Bio-One Franchise. To me, and the organization, there are multiple levels that attest to people first and business second in that business comes after the service, especially in the nature of business that we are involved in with our franchise. By being an organization that is designed and integrated to help and remedy a situation, we hold a different mindset than what other business models may follow. Let's take for example an electrician business or a plumber; when an electrician or plumber comes to your home, one of the first items that are discussed is that of payment- how much is this service or product going to cost?

With Bio-One, we look at assisting clients first, and then taking care of the "business" logistics. The last thing that a client wants to hear or talk about during a time of high stress is something that will cause even more stress or victimization to a situation where they have already been placed as a victim. By helping to provide immediate solutions and working to remedy a situation that has occurred we have designed a business model to avoid re-victimizing and ensure that the clients' needs are taken care of first and foremost.

When we are the "last responders" to a situation that has occurred, our organization brings something new to the family and client that has become a victim of a situation- we bring comfort and peace of mind. By helping to make a home feel like a situation has never happened, we create the ability to put minds at ease when the next thought process for clients then transitions to being able to rebuild their lives and grasp emotions that may be in a whirlwind after a given incident. It is our goal, not to focus on the business, but on the people impacted and immediately help to make a positive impact on their lives.

So, when an electrician or plumber is giving a quote, we are helping to immediately resolve a situation, meeting the needs of the individual client, and then taking care of the business side of things later, often with the insurance company to further alleviate stress and emotions that have been developed by the client.

Local, Regional, National and International

As a franchisee candidate, a part of the decision you are working on making for the determination as to which franchise you will be investing in is the decision of location and scope of franchise marketability and existence. Some franchise opportunities, such as McDonald's, are located across the globe, whereas other franchise opportunities are in a more infant stage and may only be currently based within a local or regional market. The decision of becoming a franchisee should have weighted importance held with location and marketability of a given franchise, in that the fortified and successful demonstration of a franchise in multiple locations spanning geography and cultures helps to illustrate the level of success that the franchise may be able to maintain into the future. In contrast, if a franchise that you are researching as a potential franchisee has only been successful within one market, or has not been tested across various regions, it may be much more of a risky investment as compared to a franchise that has maintained some degree of success in various locations.

In addition to being portrayed as a success measure, the availability of franchising opportunities for a given business can allow for you to meet the personal goals and visions that you hold in your leadership outlook. As a leader of your own career path as a franchisee, you have different freedoms to expand or create market positions with various franchise opportunities. With this ideal in mind, of local versus national versus international franchising, I would recommend that you think closely about where you see yourself as a leader moving forward- do you want to be in a specific state or region of the United States, or do you see yourself moving internationally?

Make sure that the focus is in consideration of where you see yourself with a franchise, not only in being a potential for success on paper, but also a location that suits your personal interests and vision for the future. This decision may also involve family members and friends, so communication with these stakeholders in the franchise will also be important to create lasting success with the organization that you choose to be a part of. One of the worst things that I could potentially envision as a Chief Executive Officer of an organization is that my best leaders and franchisees within the organization are unhappy with the business due to the location they are in- I want franchisees to be happy with the location, or locations, that they conduct business in. A franchise location locality should be somewhere that you could be able to consider a home and should be welcoming.

The legalities of local versus national versus international can also be a varying consideration as a potential franchisee. Paperwork and the logistics of establishing business and getting up and running can already seem to be daunting at times as a franchisee candidate, so if the franchise that is being considered is to be located in a distant state or within an international region, it will be critical to take into consideration the added legality that will take place in the process and additional requirements that may need to be upheld within the process of getting business into motion. With this information in mind, if you are set on moving into a specific state or country to begin conducting business as a franchise, ensure that the costs are measured and evaluated, and not only the numeric-value costs.

Importance of Gathering Franchise Information

Making a decision that can impact the rest of your life is one that needs to be accompanied by thorough research. A decision to go into business as a franchisee or entrepreneur should be carefully evaluated with all options weighed and formulated in the attempt to make the best decision possible that is in alignment with your goals and vision that you have for your future. This process of gathering information extends past the potential business models and franchise options available and would extend to include your personal interests and passions as this is an investment in you as well.

A great example to look at as a comparison to the process of gathering information to start a business is the decision to buy a primary home or residence and the process involved in making that decision. Before ever making the final decision and offer to purchase a certain property, you should have most likely visited several residences that you were considering, where you evaluated each of the alternatives and options available in the market that met a base criteria for what you were looking for. During the process of viewing residences, you most likely took advice and input from a realtor as well as individuals in the community to gain a feel for certain neighborhoods or schools involved; not to mention the amount of input and knowledge shared by family members or close friends that added valuable information to the equation. Then, once a potential property was decided upon, the information gathering process continued with an inspection conducted on the property that helped to determine any potential harms or repairs that needed to be attended to before the final transaction took place. Only after all of these considerations have been met and additional steps made to gather information did you make the final decision and action to purchase the property.

Much like buying a home or residence, the process of investing in a franchise and becoming a franchisee requires the ability to gather sufficient information to make an informed and impactful decision. To help make this process easier for you in your journey, let's take a look at some of the key pieces of information you should consider before selecting a franchise. When considering the below topics of information, create a checklist or spreadsheet that will allow you to compare and sort through the franchise options that you are taking into account.

When I first started out in developing the Bio-One organization, gathering information was incredibly important, not only to myself but being able to create success within the business model itself. In the business that we have, in cleaning various situations that require due diligence in handling blood and bodily fluids, there was a new level of learning that had to be first accomplished at the onset, and then carried forward with training that is now given to franchisees within the organization. But this all started out with information gathering.

By being able to gather enough information in the beginning, it made everything else easier. For example, being able to explain to my family and to the families of those that I have been able to assist throughout the past two decades in Bio-One, it is about helping first, and then doing the business aspects. I wanted, from the beginning, to ensure that we were conducting our business in the right way and taking care of people within the communities we are a part of.

Information gathering helps to breed additional success within any organization and has been a proven model to follow as based on the success developed at Bio-One.

Ask for a FDD

At the foundation of gathering information about a potential franchise, a candidate should always ask for what is known as the Franchise Disclosure Document, or FDD. You may have also heard of the document being referred to as the Uniform Franchise Offering Circular, of UFOC, if you had research completed or knowledge of franchises before 2007 when the Federal Trade Commission made the transition to FDD.

The Federal Trade Commission has developed the requirement that all franchisors must release a Franchise Disclosure Document to all franchise candidates at least 14 days prior to signing any contracts of the franchise or collecting any investment or money. The Financial Disclosure Document has been created for the purpose of being able to disclose the pertinent information available about the franchisor and the potential offering that helps to give inquiring franchisees the opportunity to make an educated decision. The Franchise Disclosure Document represents over twenty items that help to disclose relevant information that will yield an educational and informed decision by a potential franchisee on whether or not to pursue the organization further. Items within the FDD include identifying categories such as the business experience of key individuals within the franchise, initial franchise fee, estimated initial investment, territory, trademarks, contracts, and much more.

If nothing else is considered, within the document there are two critical items that should be considered by potential franchisees- Item 19 and Item 20. Item 19 within the Franchise Disclosure Document provides what is known as an earnings claim and financial performance representation where material facts based on the franchise are disclosed to potential buyers. Within item 19, a sample size is identified that presents the amount of earnings claimed by a given percentage of franchisees as well as the average incomes of franchisees within the organization. Be wary, however, that the average income representation in a Franchise Disclosure Document may be skewed based on the wide range of income reported by franchisees within the organization. In addition to average income and sample size, Item 19 also relates geographic relevance for franchise performance, helping to identify income trends based on locations, as well as franchisee background information, helping to identify skills and experiences yielded by current franchisees.

The next critical item to consider in the FDD, Item 20, helps to provide the names and contact information for current and past franchisees of the organization that helps to provide first-hand accounts of the organization; additionally, Item 20 within the FDD provides the total amount of franchise locations, sales, and closures between franchisees. This section of the FDD can be helpful in determining areas of concern or problems within a franchise if there are a large number of terminated, non-renewed, or cancelled franchises listed. Another red flag that may be noticed in Item 20 would be to see multiple franchise owners within a short amount of time at a given location, meaning that there may be profitability issues in the area or that the market may not be supported for the business model. Combining together Items 19 and 20 will help you, as a potential franchisee, to gain a better understanding and full picture of how the franchise has developed character and reputation.

The FDD should be considered the "Information Bible" when it comes to understanding your options available to you for franchises and should be acquired as soon as you begin to consider a given franchise.

Return on Investment and Initial Investment Requirement

In the process of gathering information to make a decision as to pursue a franchise or not, take the time to request the average initial investment that other franchisees have made to the organization. By acquiring an average initial investment, the ability to calculate a potential return on investment can be made. The goal in this determination is to gain an understanding for the ability for the initial investment within the franchise to generate predictable returns in relation to risk involved. If the risk for the franchise is determined to be higher than average, there will be a correlation to a lower yielding return on investment by previous franchisees. This information will require research from the perspective of existing franchisees as well as a conversation with the parent company or franchisor where the investment to buy into the franchise will be made.

Similarly, the initial discovery phase and information gathering process in considering a franchise should allow you to determine average operating costs and average overhead involved with the franchise. Within operating costs, considerations should be made for costs such as labor and supplies and overhead costs such as rent and utilities should be incorporated into the information-gathering efforts. By gaining as much financial data possible, a franchisee candidate can work to make a more informed decision as to whether or not to pursue the organization further based on the probability of success.

Success Rate

What has been the average success rate for past franchisees? As a franchisee candidate, make an effort to understand how many franchise locations have closed or failed in the past, and determine what the underlying reasons were for the failed franchise locations. If you are considering multiple franchise options, developing a success rate equation for each option can be helpful in making the final decision. To create a success rate equation, simply divide the number of closed franchise locations by the number of total open franchise locations to determine what the success rate has been for the organization.

As an example for comparing success rates to make a decision as to where to invest as a franchisee, let's consider a hypothetical situation where you are considering Franchise A versus Franchise B. Franchise A has had a total of 100 locations open within the past 10 years, and of that total, 5 locations have closed their doors due to economic decline. The Success Rate for Franchise A would be calculated as follows: 5 (Failed Locations) / 100 (Total Open) = 5%, then calculate 100% - 5% = 95%. This means that Franchise A has a 95% Success Rate.

Considering the same example, let's say that Franchise B has opened a total of 75 locations in the past ten years, and of the 75 opened, 7 have had to close due to various reasons. Using the same Success Rate calculation as above, the rate for Franchise B would be calculated as follows: 7 (Closed Locations) / 75 (Total Opens) = 9.33%, (100% - 9.33% = 90.6% Success Rate).

After comparing the Success Rate of Franchise A (95%) and Franchise B (90.6%), a franchisee candidate can make a more informed decision as to which franchise to invest in, leaning toward Franchise A based on a higher rate of success. This, of course, is only one piece of information as a part of the entire picture of making a decision, but can help add a quantitative aspect to decision making that can seem overwhelming and hard to narrow down top perspective franchise options.

Fee and Cost Structures

How much will you need to invest within the franchise and what additional costs are associated? To make an informed decision that is most beneficial as a franchisee candidate, you should begin to identify and study any and all fees and costs that are associated to a given franchise. When considering fees and costs involved, ensure that you include not only the initial fees that are required to buy-into a franchise, but dig deeper to determine continuing fees, equipment fees, industry-specific fees such as food costs, post-term fees, advertising and marketing fees, penalty fees, and anything else that you can get your hands on to determine the true cost of ownership. Unfortunately, many franchise options available seem like a great or low-cost investment option in the beginning, but hidden fees and costs sneak up and make the long term investment much more costly than originally anticipated. These hidden fees and costs should be considered as a red flag as some franchise organizations throughout the world have been developed for the purpose to profit from franchisee costs imposed with the purchase of specialized equipment or food that is used for the franchise. My advice when it comes to hidden costs and fees is if something looks and sounds too good to be true, it probably is and there might be additional costs involved, so do your research and recognize early that the lowest franchise royalties does not necessarily equate to the most profitable options.

Franchise Support

One of the items that intrigues most people to consider a franchise as compared to starting a business from scratch is the support and framework provided to help lead to success. I am willing to bet that if I invited you to join a franchise but didn't provide any type of support in the form of training, marketing, or technology, and still expected a franchise royalty, you would probably be upset and would not be invested in creating much success. I am willing to say this, because if I were presented in the same situation, I would walk away and never have a second thought of consideration. The basis for support given by a franchise is a critical component in the information-gathering phase of becoming a franchisee and should be overarching to include support for initial training, construction specialization if needed, grand opening support, marketing and advertising, technology, ongoing support services, and much more. As a determining factor of whether or not to consider investing within a franchise, ensure that you understand the level of support given to franchisees based on the amount of initial franchise investment, and consider what is your personal expectation for the amount of support that you would expect in order to succeed in the business venture as this expectation can be different from person to person.

Communication

Similar to the expectation of support, there should also be a consideration made to how much communication is shared and built upon between franchisor and franchisee. A great way to determine the strength of communication within a potential franchise is to directly contact a franchisee and discuss what their personal level of satisfaction has been with the franchisor. Even better than a current franchisee, if possible, speak with a former franchisee and ask about how the level of communication was within the franchise as well as what the relationship seemed to be like between franchisor and franchisee. Above and beyond contacting current and past franchisees, determine if there is any participation in a franchisee association as this can be an indicator of a healthy franchise system that has been developed and can add to the consideration you are making in deciding between multiple franchise investment options.

Economically Sound

In this section, let's take a snapshot from the world of finance and investment with looking at finding the best possible franchise options as a franchisee candidate. In finance and investment strategies, one will often hear the term of "Beta" being referred to in many discussions. The idea of Beta is a numeric value that is applied to every stock and investment option that is publicly traded on exchanges such as NASDAQ and NYSE. The value of Beta is a representation of how the performance of a given stock will deviate in comparison to market performance.

Historical examples of very strong Beta-performance companies would be that of Budweiser and McDonald's, where their Beta is viewed as being low, and having minimal deviation from overall market performance and being identified as recession-resistant organizations. The idea being here, when times are "good" (high stock market and economic performance) people will drink beer and when times are bad (low market performance or minimal economic drivers) people will drink beer; additionally, when times are good people will eat McDonalds and when times are bad people will eat McDonalds.

In contrast, historical examples of high Beta's such as Apple Inc, or Sony, that are volatile based on economic trends and demand in the marketplace make the stocks more of an unpredictable performing stock when adding into an investment portfolio.

These stocks may pay high dividends, but there is also considerably more risk involved for short term investments and related options.

An investor looking to avoid stocks and options that are highly unpredictable with market performance and are looking for a solid long-term investment strategy will lean toward an investment with a low Beta value, or one that has demonstrated lower volatility over the life of the stock's performance. This same idea can be applied when looking for a franchise investment opportunity as a franchisee candidate- looking for a franchise that is succession proof.

Regions throughout the United States and throughout the globe have demonstrated unique economic trends and should be considered as a part of the franchise consideration experience. The economy is a cycle that tends to have repeating factors. Look back to 2008 or the early 1990's to late 1980's and think of how some franchise options would have performed with weakened economies. When considering your choice of a franchise, think of how sales performance would be impacted based on the purchasing power of the individuals within the community that you will be participating in. This process should go beyond a macro-level and look closer at strong economic drivers in the specific region that you are looking to perform as a franchise.

Taking economic indicators beyond a macro, or national, level and looking closer to a local level, one can attribute factors that may cause additional volatility and threats, or opportunities, to a given franchise model. Again, looking back to the "Great Recession of 2008," some markets throughout the United States were considerably more challenged than others when looking at economic performance, such as with the Detroit, Michigan area where auto sales performance and housing market devaluation caused tremendous negative impacts to the community and surrounding businesses. In contrast, markets such as Denver, Colorado were impacted at a much lower level during the recession, keeping job performance and housing at a much steadier level as compared to Detroit.

Is there a main economic driving engine within the community or region that you are looking to pursue a franchise? In your consideration of available franchise options, estimate a numeric value similar to that of Beta to each franchise that you are considering, and put an estimate as to how much you feel the business model would be impacted by potential changes within the national and local economies, or even globally. If you find that the potential franchise will have significant changes in performance if there is a change in the economy, then that may identify a potential threat and may be considered as a less likely candidate to pursue as compared to other options that are less likely to be highly impacted with this volatility faced. There will undoubtedly be changes in all economies, both locally and nationally, into the future and it is important to make a decision of a franchise that will work with you on each of the changes, not against you.

Quality in Product and Service

All too often, I hear or personally see franchisees that join a franchise without truly understanding the product or service that is being provided. If you have never traveled, why would you sell luggage, or if you are a vegetarian, why would you sell hamburgers? To be successful in a franchise, you need to have a strong understanding for what the product or service being offered truly is and it is equally important to find a franchise that offers a superior product or service that has demonstrated success in a wide range of economic and market environments. Also, determine what the level of service has been at existing franchises and what is the perception of the organization within the community, specifically citing if there is a long history of litigation related to the franchise. Litigation information would be disclosed within the Franchise Disclosure Document and should be considered closely in relation to the perception of the organization within communities.

Continuing on the idea of perception, the brand that has been developed by a franchise says a lot about the potential organizations being considered. Based on your information gathering, have you been able to determine whether or not a franchisor has worked hard to develop integrity and quality within the brand and have you also been able to determine what the brand communicates? Quality, integrity, and consistency should be benchmarks to demand when it comes to choosing a franchise because a brand and company name reflects to success. If a brand is perceived by customers or associations in a positive light, then that positivity will reflect in the ability to maintain sales, advertising strategies, future funding, etc. etc. A brand can either make or break an organization and the perception of the franchise should be evaluated in your comparison between options available.

In addition to the items listed above, there are multiple other considerations that can be included in your decision as to which franchise to pursue. Each item should be considered and closely evaluated independently, and be sure to include any personal considerations that align with your individual values to make the comparison specific to you as you understand what is most important, not someone else. Consider items separately, but look for patterns and correlations between items to help develop a summative understanding for each option. The more information and understanding you have, the easier it will be to make a decision.

Selecting from Options

Weighing the options as a franchisee candidate at this point can be incredibly challenging for some, as making a decision at this point may mean success or failure for years to come. There is a lot of information that has been analyzed up to this point, and will continue to be analyzed moving forward even after selecting the final franchise to pursue. To make it easier in the process of selecting from available options, we will now take a look at several ideas to consider when making a decision in pursuing a franchise.

Every decision that is made is made with the consideration of certain factors being more weighted as compared to other factors. This is completely understandable as every leader, business owner, individual, and franchisee has a unique set of values and perspective on what is most important to him or her. With the ideal in mind that unique factors and values may be more important than others, the first option available to pursue when making a decision will be in consideration of this weighted decision making process.

Completing the decision making process with a weighted method first requires you, as a potential franchisee candidate, to understand your personal values and degree of importance for perspective that you align in your personal life. Take, for example, that you value working with a certain group of people or value working with a dynamic situation placed on one's life-you may need to consider this as a weighted factor when making a decision. Additionally, if you have the goal of living in a certain state or specific region of the country, a weighted perspective should be given toward being with a franchise that allows you to be within the region or location that is most positive or beneficial to you.

To create an effective weighted measure when making a decision as to which franchise to pursue, begin with making a list of the top priorities that you maintain as an individual. Some of the considerations that you can consider could be similar to the following, or include the following:

- If you were to do something and not be paid for it, but enjoy every minute, what would it be?
  - Evaluate all the tasks and activites you will be performing every single day. Would you enjoy doing those activities? Now imagine you would not get paid for it, would you still appreciate those tasks? This can give you a strong idea of where to pursue a franchise. There are countless franchise opportunities throughout the world, such as Bio-One, that allow for the consideration of personal values and priorities, and by doing something that you enjoy while also making a career will be an incredible find.
- What skill or experience set do you consider to be your highest level of expertise or most comfortable ability?
  - When considering your top franchise option, you not only want to be able to find a good fit as to a location and opportunity that you enjoy being a part of, but you also want to find a franchise where your skills and experiences will be maximized. By finding a weighted measure to factors related to your personal experience and comfort level based on previous skills acquired, you will be more apt to be successful within the organization going forward. Within the realm of franchise options, the ability to find an organization that correlates to your experiences, the more the chance for sustainability and profitability to occur. The idea of finding correlating experiences does not have to be one-for-one in the sense that similar experiences and skills can be cross-referenced to maintain success within the organization.

A great example of cross-referencing skills and experience is found with Bio-One and the Franchisees that lead and guide within the organization each and every day. Most franchisees that take part in Bio-One have never cleaned a crime scene or site before taking part in the organization, but their ability to direct relatable experiences helps to create a high degree of success within the business model. Experiences developed as an individual before venturing into a franchise, such as relationship building, sales, and customer service can be directly related to the strengths required when building a successful franchise. So, even though a franchisee at Bio-One may have never had an exact experience with a crime scene or general cleanup situation, does not mean that they cannot be incredibly successful with the amount of experiences that directly relate to the position required. Leaders come in a wide variety with incredible experiences that add value to unique situations within Bio-One; if you can bring the leadership, we will supply the details and help you to succeed in the franchise.

Using the weighted measure to identify a high quality selection of franchise, such as Bio-One, is suitable for a great majority of franchisee candidates, but there are other considerations to be made as well, such as quantitative factors.

Quantitative factors, including cost of ownership in a franchise, are often a primary factor in determining which business model will be the final option to move forward with. There are multiple perspectives of cost when reviewing a potential franchise, including a franchise fee, licenses and permits required, insurance, and any additional equipment and advertising costs required for initial franchise development. The commonly coined phrase, "it takes money to make money" comes into view with any franchise, but it is vital to get a potential for return of investment within the franchise you select. Taking into consideration the availability of funds that may be available for franchise development may be at the top of the selection factor, in that you will want to pursue a franchise that is at a reasonable level, or within your business-means of pursuit. If a franchise seems too costly, either in comparison to available funding, or in comparison to competing franchise options, it may be important to consider another high performing franchise option. This brings us to the next level of making a selection between available options- performance and ranking between competing franchises.

Selecting between the top two or three franchises that you have derived as a part of the determination process up to this point may require outside perspective. Enlisting the assistance for measure and decision from a third-party perspective or a neutral party may be highly valuable in the process that you are currently pursuing. A neutral perspective may come from a past colleague or group of peers that can work to make an unbiased selection or insight as to more specifics to help make the final decision easier. Additionally, information gained from third-party rating sources, such as National rating organizations or Better Business Bureau reviews may be of high value and consideration in the process. The benefit of adding third-party perspective and ratings may add an additional quantitative perspective on the final decision when narrowing down between the top two or three.

From a weighted measure of selection among options, to enlisting the assistance of a third-party source, the final decision may not be able to be made until an in-person review and one-on-one meeting is fulfilled. We will continue to walk through reviewing franchise options as well as the benefits of working with Bio-One, but I can consistently say, with confidence, that working with Bio-One every franchisee candidate receives the opportunity and utmost value in conducting one-on-one meetings and interviews with myself as well as leaders within the organization to help provide a full perspective on the benefit of working as a part of the business model.

Let's take a closer look at additional factors that help to make Bio-One the best choice for incoming franchisees looking for sustainable success in available business models.

Why Bio-One is the Best Option

As a franchisee candidate and one seeking to continue to grow and develop in a potential venture, it is imperative to be able to understand the process of selecting from franchise choices available as well as how to effectively critique options before being able to appreciate why Bio-One stands out as the best opportunity available. Throughout this book, you have the opportunity to receive an unique insight into Bio-One and the reasons as to why some of the top franchisees in the industry have said why they feel Bio-One is the "best" option available to franchisee candidates; however, in this section, I want to take a moment and walk through the franchise process with Bio-One and help to illustrate why, at the structural element, Bio-One is considered the best possible choice for a franchisee.

In the research that you have conducted already on potential franchise options available, how many have you found with an "Open-door" policy on their website? I am providing an educated guess that most of the franchise options that you have looked at have required you to get past an electronic "gate keeper" and request additional information to get straight forward answers in regards to important decision factors such as costs and structure of becoming a franchisee with the organization. At Bio-One, I am proud to be able to say that we provide an "Open-Door" policy from the first click on the website. Take a look for yourself, check the website at http://www.biooneinc.com/franchise-process.html and http://www.biooneinc.com/requirements.html and you will see what an open-door franchise looks like. Because of the unique nature that crime and trauma bring to our work flow model, we continually develop a unique perspective toward franchises that many other business models do not consider following. We take a conscious perspective that we do not want to waste time by not sharing adequate information necessary to a potential franchisee candidate, and feel that it is our responsibility to

42

help potential franchisees to have enough information to make the best decision for them. This is why we are so adamant about having our "Open-door" of information available at every point of the process of becoming a franchisee at Bio-One. This is where success starts with Bio-One.

From the first perspective of research conducted with Bio-One, you are able to effectively determine what the process will look like, from the first phone call with me to beginning training as a franchisee. If you have not already determined by the basis of this book, one of my primary goals for potential franchisees is that he or she knows and is aware of all available information that can help to form a decision that will positively impact their lives as well as an honest assessment of what their lives will look like as a franchisee, whether it be with Bio-One or another organization that they choose to embark upon.

I will be the first to say that Bio-One is not for everyone and it is critical to find a mutually beneficial relationship among any potential franchisee; however, I do feel that there is tremendous value in sharing the vision and benefits of Bio-One with you as a top consideration to help you succeed into the future.

In the previous section, we discussed finding a franchise that is essentially recession-proof or less volatile with changes in the economy. Examples of Budweiser and McDonalds were identified as historically favored investment options for investors that are looking to reduce their volatility in the stock market, showing that when the economy is either strong or weak, individuals pursue purchases with both organizations along the full spectrum, making them strong investment options. This same ideal is maintained with Bio-One as a franchise that has been identified as being recession proof.

The nature of Bio-One's business functions is to help support individuals in need after situations that cause the need for emergency cleaning, medical waste disposal, odor removal, mold remediation, rodent dropping cleanup, sewage backup cleanup, hoarding cleanup, decomposition cleanup, blood cleanup, and a full range of additional spectrum of accident-related cleanup. When times are good, these situations will occur, and when the economy is struggling, these situations that require an emergency and experienced service of cleanup will be necessary. For this reason, Bio-One can be considered a top choice in franchising to support the needs of a recession-proof franchise and one that will stand the test of time. Why gamble with the economy when you can guarantee opportunities to apply business functions and client relationships with Bio-One in all performance metrics of the economy.

The next factor evaluated in helping to determine a top quality franchise that is worth investing in as a franchisee is that of the production of a top quality product and service. At Bio-One, the entire framework of the organization is based on the premise of providing a top quality service and product that treats people first, and then looks at the business aspect. "Help first, business second" is more than a simple phrase of words, it is the culture that we develop and create in the relationships between clients and team members each and every day we walk onto a job site and get down to business. It is the ability to create personable relationships with clients that have been victims in one way or another, ensuring that we do not ever re-victimize them, and build upon these relationships established to create mutually beneficial success. By reaching past the business aspect of a franchise, and truly helping to solve critical needs for clients, that allow us to say that we are one of the best franchises available today.

If you are looking for the bottom line proof of why Bio-One is the best franchise to invest in as a potential franchisee, look no further than 100 percent success to date. It is practically impossible to find another franchise that can stake the claim that they have attributed to 100 percent success rate for franchisees that have invested within the organization. It is nearly impossible, but Bio-One is not the norm, we have been able to prove that we are one of the best. The success of a franchise is the highest goal that I maintain as a Chief Executive Officer, and I am able to convey that success does not come without an investment in the individuals that lead the franchise- you as a potential franchisee.

At Bio-One, we limit franchise expansion to 12-15 per year. By limiting franchise expansion, we are able to more fully invest in the success of incoming franchisees by being able to devote over 1000 hours of training into each incoming franchisee per year. The ability to have a primary and heavy focus on training and investment in the development of leaders within the organization is what helps to build the 100 percent success model that we have maintained; this makes us different and sets us apart from the franchise models that take on 20 or more franchises throughout any given month, causing the inability to provide fundamental support and training. It is the individualized approach that we maintain and that we develop through a sustainable training model that helps to make us different and helps to make Bio-One one of the best franchise opportunities available in the United States and perhaps the world today.

Let's take a look at some of the tools and services that are available for you to become the best franchisee and leader within an organization possible, hopefully as a future leader within the best franchise option currently available in the United States-Bio-One.

Developing a Foundation of Investors and Financing

When looking to invest in any type of business venture, ranging from a franchise to starting as a Sole Proprietorship, the basis and understanding that it "takes money to make money" must be realized. The sooner those individuals are able to comprehend the idea that it truly takes an investment to pay dividends, the sooner they can become successful. When I first started out with the development of Bio-One, after spending years in the corporate realm, there was an initial nervousness felt and caution in that I knew I was taking a risk, but the more that I think about the process now, I think I would have been more concerned if I didn't sense the level of risk. The excitement and nerves that build when thinking about going into business for yourself is a good thing- it means that you care. If you didn't care, then that would be a concern.

It is ok to have some feelings of nervousness when it comes to thinking about investing in yourself and the organization that you are working to establish through franchising, but they must be overcome with the realization that it is this investment that will carry you forward. After realizing that an investment is necessary, the ability to generate funds for the investment is found as the next critical step in the process. There are multiple options in developing a foundation of investors and we will look at those options here as well as other ideas to help provide the initial investment that is needed to jump start a franchise.

Commercial Lending

The first place that many franchisees turn to when looking at jump starting a franchise with funding is at commercial banks. Throughout history, commercial banks have been recognized for their ability to lend to franchisees and can be a stable source of funds that are provided at a set term and made available within a relatively short amount of time. When considering looking at financing with a commercial bank, one of the biggest considerations that are viewed from the perspective of the financial institution is that of your credit rating. With a lending application for franchising, a commercial bank will most certainly ask for a complete loan package that includes personal financial statements, records of personal tax returns for multiple years, and verification from what will be a down payment. Commercial banks and business lending programs often require down payments of at least 20 percent, so this is an additional consideration when thinking about building a foundation of financing and investment going into a franchise.

When commercial banks look at the potential for lending to franchisees, additional determinations are made on the basis of the franchise itself. A commercial bank will look toward brands and franchises that have demonstrated a track record of success that have provided positive cash flows in other establishments, rather than franchise ventures that have been in existence for shorter periods of time or with fewer locations as they have provided a lack of proof that they can perform well in multiple regions and in varying economic conditions.

When considering Bio-One and similar franchise options, franchisees can be assured of high performance and early achieving break-even-points with positive cash flow. With commercial banks favoring businesses with this consistency, it is important to make your top choice of a franchise system is one that will help, and not hinder, your vision. For franchisees that have the availability of funds for down payment options or reasonable collateral availability, looking at the route of commercial lending can be a valuable resource when creating the development of initial investment for a franchise. But what about those franchisees that still want structure with investment and financing toward the franchise but don't have the available down payment or have not have been able to establish a lengthened relationship with a commercial banker or limited credit experience in business? That's where SBA Lending comes in.

U.S. Small Business Administration (SBA) Lending

Another example of business investment strategy and initial financing for a franchisee is looking toward the route of the U.S. Small Business Administration, or SBA, Lending channel. SBA loans are different than commercial lending options in that they are partially guaranteed by the United States government and help to illustrate a level of reduced risk when considering lending options. There is a standard loan option made available by the Small Business Administration that is most often suitable for franchisees and is known as the 7(a) SBA Loan. A 7(a) SBA loan option is one that is issued by a bank or financial institution and is additionally guaranteed against default by the United States government, helping to reduce the risk for the institution and providing the ability of lending to become more widely available for individuals looking to start out with a franchise or other new business ventures.

SBA lending options also provide a different range of payback and loan-purpose options as compared to commercial lending. SBA lending has equipment-specific loans and short-term working capital lending options that have shorter maturities within five to six years and can be extremely valuable for an individual seeking supportive financing when starting a franchise. Additionally, real-estate loans that have a range up to 20-year paybacks with SBA lending give peace of mind to financing for multiple locations and storefronts that are the entry way for many clients into the organization.

Historically, SBA Loans have been very supportive of franchisees, with average loans between $250,000 - $500,000 that help franchisees to finance entry fees and working capital that help to establish and sustain a franchise in the early years of operation. Additionally, SBA lending options normally have a variable interest rate that are tied to the prime rate and can fluctuate based on qualifications of the borrower. To qualify for SBA lending, a franchisee must be able to demonstrate that they are credit worthy and sometimes require a contribution of equity. The repayment of SBA loans, similar to that of commercial lending will be directly associated to the franchise cash flows and will be set at structured terms of repayment.

Veteran Lending Option through SBA

First and foremost, I would like to take a moment and thank those that sacrifice all and have worked to protect the freedoms that we enjoy in the United States, both in the past, present and into the future, and if you are reading this book and have either served in the past or currently served in the Armed Forces, I would like to continue to extend my sincere thanks and gratitude. As the Chief Executive Officer of Bio-One, and as an individual that has been involved with multiple organizations throughout my personal career, some of the best franchisees that I have come across are those that have served in the military and the U.S. Small Business Administration has maintained the same attitude.

Under the Small Business Administration lending program there is a special program known as the Patriot Express that is conducted in partnership with the Department of Veterans Affairs. The Patriot Express is a government lending program that has been recognized for exceptionally fast approval times as compared to other lending channels and allows for financing up to $500,000 to active-duty and veteran military personnel that are making the transition to civilian life and are looking to start a business. Additionally, the Patriot Express program is available to spouses and survivors of veterans and provides the lowest rates possible through the SBA Lending program. The values upheld by those that have served in the military and the experiences gained reflect directly in becoming influential and successful franchise owners and the availability of funding to start out a franchise could not be better.

Private/Group Investing

The next option that individuals primarily look at for investing within a franchise and determining a funding strategy to start out is to look at private investment or group investment options. Let's say that you have not had the opportunity to develop a relationship with a commercial banking lender or have not had the ability to develop a sufficient amount of equity that would be involved or asked upon for commercial lending or SBA lending options; that is where private investing or group investing would come in. Rather than going to the commercial bank down the street or online for financing, you would look to create interest among peer business owners and leaders that you are close to in your community, or even within your own family, to develop the amount of financing necessary to take on a franchise opportunity.

The option of private and group investing has both positive and negative attributes. On the positive end of the spectrum, private and group lending provides an extraordinary amount of flexibility. Essentially, if you can think it or dream it, private investing can be molded to your needs depending on the availability of funding. Customization within private lending can range in dollar amounts provided as well as payback terms. When commercial lending and SBA lending options have structured payback periods, often with monthly due dates, private lending will most likely be much more flexible and provide options such as quarterly payments, every-other month, or even more flexible payment options such as future re-payments after break-even point. The ability to be exceptionally flexible with financing a franchise is the key benefit for private lending.

At first glance, private lending and group lending options may seem like a sure-fire bet to having a successful start at becoming a franchisee; however, there are a few considerations to take into account that may not fit every business model. Private and group lending only allows for enough funds that you are able to seek out or feel comfortable asking. If there is a downturn in business and repayment becomes challenging for any reason, the individuals often sought for private financing are close friends and family and this relationship may cause emotional turmoil if things go negative for any reason. There is flexibility involved, but the personal connections in private lending channels may not be best for everyone. I will let you make that call.

Individual Investment and Funding

If you are anything like me, you spent your time in the corporate world, building up the 401(k) week after week, living day-by-day hoping and wondering what would happen into the future, and knowing that the corporate world and working for someone else was not truly what you were meant to be doing. But even though the environment you are in is not where you want to continue to be, you have probably had the ability to begin building up a solid nest-egg in the form of a 401(k) or IRA and can consider using funds from these accounts in pursuit of developing a franchise. In addition to 401(k) and IRA disbursements, you can also look at personal credit options such as Home Equity Loans or Lines of Credit that can give you additional flexibility and initial financing options to pursue a franchise.

The key to finding the best approach to investing and financing for a franchise is to look inward and move outward. What I mean by this is, first, look at your own personal situation and the strengths that you maintain and the opportunities that you may have within your network or personal assets that can be used to develop financing for the franchise that you are looking to pursue. From that point, after analyzing your individual situation, you can move forward with private lending, commercial lending, SBA lending, or a combination of multiple options to begin meeting the vision that you have set.

The main point that I want to bring across in this section is that there are many options to help begin to finance and invest in your dream to become a franchisee, and every option should be equally considered and thought over to work to meet the goals that you have set.

For additional information on franchise lending options and business lending, here are a few resources that I recommend checking out:

- https://www.treasury.gov/resource-center/sb-programs
- www.sba.gov
- www.kabbage.com
- www.businesslenders.com

Making a Decision

In the end, after all of the information has been gathered and information has been developed to coordinate available options, a decision must be made. You are getting ready to make one of the most important decisions in your life as this next decision may spark the next career and path that you will be following. As seen in the previous sections, there is an incredible amount of information to consider when making a decision as to which franchise to pursue. To assist in this process, take some time to yourself and create a system for organizing and prioritizing your thoughts and information gained in the research process.

Making a final decision is more of an art form than a science, but by being able to be more organized and take into account weighted measures that you have uncovered, you will be able to make a more insightful decision as to where to go forward with a franchise. Next up, you will be provided a Self-Assessment that may also assist in this process of finalizing a decision as to where you will be focusing your energy and personal investment into the next chapter of your life as a business leader. It is an exciting time and a time where more information may be needed to make the final decision, so let's continue the journey and help to uncover additional ideas and recommendations to make this next journey a successful one- no matter which decision you make.

Self-Assessment

At this point in the process, you have the ideas in your mind as to where you will most likely be into the future in relation to given franchise options. In this Self-Assessment, the goal is to help provide a spectrum of importance related to the factors that you hold important as a business leader and potential franchisee. Attempt to clear your mind, go through each of the questions and answer as best as possible how you feel in regard to the question being presented. After completing the assessment, go back and review the results and see if there are any additional discoveries that you may have made about yourself and where you may want to lean towards in making a final decision as to which franchise to pursue.

Using a Rating Scale of 1 to 5, with 1 being "Do Not Agree/ Does Not Relate" and 5 being "Agree Strongly/Relates Strongly," take note for each of the following questions:

1. If I get started on a project, I see it through until the end.

    1   2   3   4   5

2. I envision myself working in a hands-on environment as the leader of an organization.

    1   2   3   4   5

3. There is no such thing as failure, there is only the opportunity to learn.

    1   2   3   4   5

4. I can easily find financing and availability of funds to pursue my top franchise choice.

    1   2   3   4   5

5. There is no such thing as the "End of the Day."

    1   2   3   4   5

6. In the franchise that I pursue, I want to have a high level of training and support provided rather than being on my own completely.

    1   2   3   4   5

7. No job is above or below me. I am committed to do my best.

    1   2   3   4   5

8. Engaging with the public and helping my community is important to me.

    1   2   3   4   5

9. An idea can be supported by vision and hard work and can become success.

    1   2   3   4   5

10. Gaining perspective from others is important when making high impact decisions.

| 1 | 2 | 3 | 4 | 5 |

After notating your personal results from the Self-Assessment, take a moment and review additional ideas that may have stirred in your mind and take those into account when making your final decision as to which franchise to pursue. We will continue to take a closer look at the Franchise Business Model and additional options to consider, so hold this information gained close by and get ready to inspire the next positive change in your life and create success.

Franchise Business Model

Bio-One, just as with other franchise business models has been developed with a foundation of structure and processes that help to replicate success in multiple regions and markets. At its simplest form, a franchise is created with the goal of providing incentive to a franchisee as they have a greater stake in the business organization and are able to take the firm's business model and processes in place, as well as the brand, to create additional success in a new marketplace. A franchise business model creates the ability to maintain success in business without having to "reinvent the wheel" of the business.

To have access to the framework for success that a franchise provides, there are usually multiple fees that take place as well as a contractual agreement between franchisor and franchisee. There may be fees including royalty use fees for the trademark of the organization, training fees, and a percentage of individual business unit sales that are directed back to the franchisor. Often times, these fees are simplified and combined into one fee structure known as a Management Fee and should be disclosed in the Franchise Disclosure Document.

According to the International Franchise Association, over 40 percent of businesses in the United States follow the franchise business model, creating an incredible amount of opportunity and choice to think through as a potential franchisee. The business model of a franchise is a welcome idea as it helps to provide a framework for success with some degree of buy-in from a franchisee that then helps to propel heightened achievement moving forward that would have been much more challenging to achieve if conducted as a startup and without the support and integration of a bigger business model.

To gain a greater perspective on the franchise business model, let's take a look at an interview conducted with Kurt Edds, a Bio-One franchisee that has been able to work through the franchise model and create sustainable success.

Testimonial 2 – Kurt Edds, Bio-One

"If you're going through hell, keep going."
– Winston Churchill

There are going to be moments where you are ready to fly the white flag and surrender. No matter how difficult things become though, never give up on your dreams. Just keep putting one foot in front of the other and you will arrive at success.

The second testimonial featured in this book was conducted with Kurt Edds, a franchisee of Bio-One, who is a valued owner that I have had the pleasure of working with for several years. Kurt completed the interview with a third-party to help provide a neutral perspective and incorporated into this book. Kurt has been one that helps to demonstrate the qualities and personal feelings developed by leaders within Bio-One and lends great experience and personal recommendations for others. As one considering becoming a franchisee, especially with Bio-One, this is a testimonial to dive into and gain first hand perspective from an amazing leader and business owner.

Q: When did you join and why did you decide to go with such an unconventional business model?

A: Joined 3 years ago and had been in IT for 15 years. If you are familiar with IT, or at least for me, the work became unfulfilling and I was looking for something else and wanted the freedom of a business owner, but I didn't have the "business experience." I stumbled upon Bio-One and met Nick-Anthony and even before I met him, I decided that this is what I wanted to do and once I met him, it was completely solidified. I couldn't be happier- it is a different type of business- I like the variety- every day is different.

Q: Did you start by looking for Franchises to take part in?

A: I was doing internet searches and came across Bio-One. A recession-proof type industry is what caught my eye and the fact that there is a lot of business out there and it is just a matter of having an effective marketing plan, in which Nick-Anthony gives us as a part of the franchise and work to go after it to get the work. Buying into the franchise is essentially, buying a "Business in a box" because I didn't have that experience and I needed all the help I could get going into business- the websites, the help, the training, the approach- everything.

Q: You have been with Bio-One for 3 years. In that time, how has your business grown?

A: Going from 0 employees to 4 in the Denver, CO office, but I have just moved to Denver and was previously running the Dallas office and am excited to be in the area. Business is still getting off the ground and not as mature as the Dallas office, but business is growing. In fact, after this interview we have a job to go do.

Q: If someone is on the fence to go with another franchise or decide to go with Bio-One, what advice would you give them?

A: If you are looking for freedom and being a business owner and you are wanting to get out of the corporate grind and try something else and a little bit of disgusting environments don't bother you, then this is the job for you.

Q: What mindset should someone have to become a successful franchise owner?

A: You have to be very driven. The work doesn't just fall into your lap- you have to be willing to go out and get it. Being with Bio-One gives you the plan to do that.

Q: How effective do you feel the Bio-One Franchise training is to becoming successful as compared to other franchise trainings in other industries?

A: The thing that makes Bio-One different is Nick Anthony- he is a very caring Franchisor and cares about all of the offices. I don't know that you get the same family-feel that you get with other companies, but with Nick, you feel that you are part of the "family." This is something that brings a lot of individuals on board with Bio-One and we have a "Buddy System" in place for the new franchise owners/new offices and a mentor program that helps you through the entire process which is highly beneficial for those that have not been business owners in the past. With the training program at Bio-One it is very detailed and focused on the individual.

Q: What is your personal vision for Bio-One in the next five years?

A: My plan is to open a new office, but don't want to share just yet, but looking to expand and looking to do so within the next month.

Q: If someone has not been in business in the past, how do you effectively market yourself, especially as it is an unconventional business?

A: There are two options in effectively marketing their franchise. Option one, the executive model- hire salesmen to go out and do it for you. Second, and the most effective way, is for the owner to do it as you have the most on the line and it is truly your business. Nobody cares about the business more than you, so in my offices, I have always been the one to do the marketing. I love it.

Q: Nick-Anthony has 100 percent Success Rate and has not had any fail, why and how is this possible?

A: I don't think that Nick would ever let us fail. If there is a franchise that is underperforming, then that franchise will get a lot of attention to find out what the problem may be. We can give someone all the tools in the world to do the job and to sell the business, but the "drive" is something that can't be taught or instilled; this is one thing that can't be fixed, but as long as the person is out there doing it, the system and business works.

Q: Is there anything you can add to prospective Bio-One owners?

A: For anyone looking to get out of the rut and start working for themselves, the rewards that come from hard work input to the Bio-One franchise should be reason enough to give Bio-One a chance.

Additionally, the following link will allow one to gain additional insight in the successful franchise developed by Kurt Edds as a part of Bio-One: https://www.BioOneDen.com

Application Process as a Franchisee Candidate

"The secret of getting ahead is getting started."
– Mark Twain

Although it may scare you to death to begin your own franchise or business, the mere fact that you're willing to begin to work toward your goals puts you one step ahead of most others. Plus, you can't finish something until you start, so starting is definitely the key.

By now you have developed a strong understanding of some of the key fundamentals that a franchise business model holds and the primary characteristics to look for in making a decision as to which franchise you will be looking at investing in, but what happens at the next level? In this section, we will take a closer look at the application process of a franchisee, moving beyond the research phase and getting into the "what next" side of the franchise development. Using the Bio-One application process as a guide, I will now work to provide a benchmark of understanding what the next steps will look like in your immediate journey of becoming a franchisee.

Introduction to the Franchise

The first step in the franchise process of application for most organizations, including Bio-One, is the introduction to the business itself, either with an in person visit or with an introductory call. Most organizations have a department tucked away in a distant call center that attempt to provide an introductory call, but at Bio-One we operate on a much more personalized level. Every introductory call is conducted with myself, Nick-Anthony Zamucen, the Founder and Chief Executive Officer of Bio-One. As the

Founder and CEO, I find it both incredibly important and valuable to franchisee candidates to be able to review each of the tools and resources that Bio-One helps to provide as an incoming leader with the organization. In addition to being able to provide the wealth of resources available and experience from myself and other franchisees at Bio-One, the introductory call aims at being able to answer any questions that may be building in the initial outlay of becoming a franchisee. I am going to be the first one to tell you, as a franchisee candidate, to gain as much information as possible about this organization as well as any additional franchise options available for your potential investment. This needs to be a process that highlights success on both ends of the spectrum- your success equates to business success.

The introductory call with Bio-One, as well as with most franchise options available throughout the United States, is a no obligation call and is completely free. The call will allow you to gain additional perspective on the organization and help to clarify some initial pressing questions that may have arose during the preliminary research conducted. After the initial call, we send a packet of information for review and help to follow up or clarify any additional questions that may have not been able to have been answered on the initial call.

Clarifying Information and Meeting With Existing Franchisees

The next consideration in the franchisee process is a second call with myself or a Senior-franchisee with Bio-One to help answer any additional questions that may have come up since the initial call. This process is usually omitted by most franchise options available throughout the world, only relying on the first call made to help answer posing questions, which can be highly impersonal and often leaves franchisees feeling left in the dark about information that is usually pertinent to making a final decision as to invest, or not, within the given franchise. In addition, the second call grasps greater detail and information regarding the training process as a franchisee and the operations of Bio-One.

Our goal as a franchise and business is to help potential future leaders within Bio-One to have as accurate a picture of what owning and operating a franchise is actually like. To compelte this goal, the second step of the franchise application process also includes a conversation, usually in person, with a current franchisee, to help gain a clear understanding of what a "day in the life" looks like as a franchisee as well as a first-hand perspective on what others say as a part of the organization in the same role that you would soon see yourself in. Even after reading stacks of research and looking through graphs and financials, it can sometimes be literally impossible to understand the true culture and identity of a franchise unless you actually step foot into the organization and observe, first hand, the ins and outs of what the process actually entails. With an organization such as Bio-One, the ability to meet one-on-one with a current franchisee is priceless in developing a measure for success into the future, and helping to develop a greater comfort level in understanding.

If an in-person visit or phone call with existing franchisee is not initially offered by the franchise operations you are looking at being able to invest in, be sure to inquire further and be somewhat apprehensive if consideration to fill this expectation is not met.

Franchise Disclosure Document Review Meeting

As discussed in this book, the Franchise Disclosure Document (FDD) is legally required to be delivered to franchisee candidates and those inquiring further to be able to join an organization as the document helps to provide a fundamental evaluation of the organization. At Bio-One, we work to go a step further than just providing a Franchise Disclosure Document for review and set up a review meeting one-on-one with potential candidates to review the document. Again, by being able to provide the utmost in quality of information and details for each aspect of the business, we at Bio-One aim to create clear expectations of what the franchise and franchisee are agreeing to as a part of the Franchise Agreement. If unavailable in person, we can conduct the FDD review meeting over the phone, but are always willing to do what it takes to ensure every aspect of the business is reviewed in great detail and to clarify any and all expectations on both sides of the franchise equation.

The Application Itself

At this point in the application process, the actual franchise application and background check come into view. Bio-One, as well as countless other franchise organizations throughout the world have certain legal regulations and requirements to uphold as a part of the franchise agreement, and the application always includes a background check. At Bio-One, as well as with multiple other franchise options that you may be considering, maintain contracts with municipalities and government entities throughout the nation, and as a requirement of these contracts a franchisee cannot have a criminal record as a part of their background check to maintain the contract. Due to the high level of importance of maintaining valuable contracts with clients in a franchise, the aspect of having a strong application clear of criminal records is vital to the success in becoming a franchisee, not only with Bio-One, but with almost any franchise available in this day in age.

Discovery Day

The application has been submitted, the background check is complete, and all initial research has been completed with most questions clarified and answered up to this point. The next step in the process is what is normally referred to as a "Discovery Day" where primary franchise paperwork and logistics of creation are completed. At the Discovery Day at Bio-One, we bring top franchisee candidates to the training office located in Denver, Colorado and cover any additional paperwork needed as a part of the franchise requirement and help to clarify the next steps involved and additional support in creating the franchise. Additionally, as with previous stages throughout the process, we help to answer any additional questions or concerns that may have been presented as of this point.

Sign the Franchise Agreement

If you have ever gone through the process in buying a home, you will be familiar with the next step in the franchisee application process- signing the franchise agreement. This part of the process can be equated to Closing Day as part of buying a home- after signing the paperwork on this day, after exchanging an "X"-sum of funds for a Home, you receive the keys to the property and are ready to move in, full steam ahead. The day that comes where you are able to sign a franchise agreement, funds are exchanged, and you go from franchisee candidate to owning your own Bio-One Franchise, ready to conduct business and get started on the process of creating sustainability in your life and attaining the goals that you have been working so hard toward up to this point. Of course, before signing the actual franchise agreement on signing day, we want to provide you the opportunity to ask any additional questions that may have arisen up to this point and provide any additional clarifications needed.

Do you see a trend yet? If not, here it is again- knowledge and availability of information as a part of joining a franchise is incredibly important. At Bio-One, at every stage of the application process, we provide and encourage additional information to be shared and gained by franchisee candidates to provide the most adequate level of understanding of the franchise. If you are not receiving this same level of information or having information restricted for any reason at another potential franchise, this should be seen as a red flag and you should work to inquire further and have a higher degree of hesitation as to proceed further or not. If information is being withheld for any reason, this can also be a potential for franchise scams that are unfortunately in existence and should be monitored as a franchisee candidate.

Training and Implementation

After all of the logistics of paperwork and initial finances have been completed, the real process begins with training and implementation as a franchisee. At Bio-One, new franchisees attend an in-depth training school held in Denver, Colorado where certifications are achieved to allow for the process of crime scene cleanup and hazards to be handled with accuracy and safety. In addition to providing a thorough training course and certification program, at Bio-One senior level franchise, or even myself, will come to visit you in your hometown or franchise market for an on-site marketing evaluation and assistance program, grand opening process, and initial launch of the franchise. As a commitment to providing a 100 percent success franchise model, we understand that it takes hard work from both ends of the equation and we are sure not going to let you fail as a franchisee from any lack of support through training and resources available that we can provide from a home office level.

There is a wide array of franchise options available throughout the world, each of which with their own range of application processes and requirements as a franchisee candidate. Take each of the considerations into account and watch for the red flags that may arise during this process. It is during the application process that you can normally find if the leadership and management support of the organization is there to support you as a franchisee and provide a vision for your success, or you may also be able to find that they are actually in business only to support their own interests and not the interest of the franchisee. Most franchise options will find great support, but be aware of the ones that may sound too good to be true or are not providing the resources necessary to promote a successful organization.

Costs Involved

At Bio-One, we are an open book when it comes to costs involved when becoming a franchisee, but unfortunately there are many franchise options available throughout the United States and throughout the world that attempt to limit the true cost of becoming a franchisee. Some of the largest franchise options available also have a wide spectrum of startup costs and entrance fees depending on factors such as location and marketability.

One of the largest franchises in the world, Subway, can cost anywhere from $80,000 to upwards of over $250,000 to gain entrance as a franchisee. From an outside perspective looking in, this can be daunting as the factor of having an unknowing investment for inconsistent results is uneasy to consider for any business leader. This is where Bio-One makes a substantial difference in the field of developing franchise opportunities. At Bio-One, the franchise fee is maintained at a minimal $35,000 with total costs of startup and franchise buy-in totaling less than $75,000. The ability to maintain consistent structure in costs as a franchise helps potential franchisees to be more confident in developing a marketing plan and also more confident in being able to realize break-even status and enhanced profitability in a much shorter period of time as compared to other franchise options available throughout the world.

Franchisor Controls and Obligations

A franchisor is responsible for helping to protect the trademark of the organization and is the fundamental processor of developing business concepts at a macro-level and maintaining the training capability of sharing the know-how with franchisees and leaders within the organization to maintain a shareable business model. On the flip side, franchisees have the requirement to maintain the services developed in a way that promotes the trademark that has been made prominent by the franchisor. This process requires some degree of standardization, either requiring a specific range of training that develops consistency among processes and can even control the uniforms and equipment utilized in franchise locations. The ability to develop a level of standardization helps to create a pattern for success that can be replicated and followed and also allows for consistency in perception of the brand, so that if an individual seeks services and products from a franchise in Region A, and then travels to Region B and receives services once again, they will have a similar result because of the standardization maintained by the franchise.

At Bio-One, we devote over 1,000 hours of training with incoming franchisees in a full range of industry-specific courses such as HAZWOPER, HAZMAT Training, Mold Certification Training, Blood Born Pathogen Certification, Sharps Certification, and Waste Management and Control; by having a detailed core of fundamental training and by investing in the leaders of the franchise, we help to create consistency in every market we

are in. In addition to developing consistency, the enhanced training provided also creates the ability to reduce the potential for
failure and is one of the biggest reasons as to why there has not
been a single franchise within Bio-One that has not maintained
success for the past two decades. We are dedicated to not only
consistency among franchising, but we also dedicate ourselves to
investing in each of the franchisees and leaders that are a part of
the organization to be able to develop additional means for success within the organization.

Cost VS. Reward- How a Franchise Can Create Wealth

In the following section, we will be diving into how a franchise creates wealth for franchisees and will share additional recommendations on how to create sustainable wealth in franchising. We will also dive into cost analysis strategies when comparing options of franchises as well as additional decisions that will be made throughout the leadership process within any organization. First, we will start with the perspective from Bio-One and the idea of how Success Breeds Success to create positive performance and the ability to attain wealth.

Success Breeds Success Perspective

Empowering Others

❝**Do not wait to strike till the iron is hot; but make it hot by striking.**❞ – William Butler Yeats

Your future doesn't just "happen" to you; you create it, so choose to create something good. Make opportunities happen and open doors that are closed.

From the success that has been developed in industries and franchises from around the world, many individuals ask the key question of, "How do you create success?" From where I sit and view the world of corporations and international business development, one of the easiest things to say in reply is that success boils down to one common denominator- empowering others. You have read several interviews and snapshots from franchisees of Bio-One that have stated that their success is because I did not let them fail. In essence, I do not provide a magic solution to provide 100 percent success across all franchises, but rather, empower others; further, I encourage and emphasize the importance of leaders within the corporation to continue to empower others in their teams.

Think about this example for a moment, on the side of not empowering others. Let's say that you are the business owner of a Coffee Franchise and have not empowered others around you or the team that has been developed. Two weeks into the start of your franchise, your doors are open and you have a steady stream of customers walking in the door, it seems like this is going to be an immediate success; however, small issues start to arise. First, the espresso machine that was just purchased had a mechanical issue, then one of your night shift employees called out for the rest of the week due to severe illness, then multiple vendors began asking for critical information to help provide services going forward, etc. etc. By not empowering others, such as team leaders or assistant supervisors, the brief success that was felt within the first week or so of the franchise quickly wears off, and you become stretched thin, causing delays to your customers and vendors and ultimately impacting your bottom line negatively.

Sometimes it can be easy to think that you can take on the challenge of a franchise or a startup business on your own, and in some rare situations this may be in fact true, but if you are a part of the 99.9 percent of individuals with the entrepreneurial spirit that is driving you to want to succeed, then empowering others needs to be a critical element that will help create success within your business. The first idea to consider in empowering others is to not think of it as a way that you are losing power or influence within your business- that is far from the truth. In actuality, by helping to empower others within your organization, you build confidence in your team as well as a foundation of trust- both of which goes a long way in creating success within the organization.

How do you empower others within your team to create success? First, have faith in your training and communication that you have developed with your team. By spending the time necessary to adequately train your team and help them to become knowledgeable of the processes and procedures you have in place, you can help to develop a more knowledgeable team. What you put into it is what you will get out of it. If you put a high amount of emphasis into the training and development of your team in the beginning, it will help to build empowerment later. By having a knowledgeable team, this also places less stress on you as you can be confident as a leader that your team will be able to help answer questions quickly when necessary to continue to meet the needs of your clients and vendors.

Beyond having faith in training and communication with your team and developing effective training in the beginning, the next piece of the puzzle in empowering others is to set expectations and provide continual feedback. As a business owner and franchisee, there will be hundreds of tasks that will need attention and application, but only so much time in the day. By empowering others with setting expectations, you can help to minimize the overload of assignments placed solely on you. Assign specific roles and tasks within your team and give them the freedom to complete them. Provide a given timeline as to when you expect the completion of the activities and what you expect as to the results, and then come back to the assignment and provide feedback when completed. After the task is completed by your team, have a conversation with them, either providing recognition or constructive feedback on how to improve next time.

Continual feedback, through recognition and coaching, is critically important in the stage of creating an empowered team. Feedback, either positive or negative, is not something that should be given only once or twice a year, or even monthly, but rather, should be given on a daily basis with the team that you work with. The only way to continue to improve and build an empowered team that you will be confident in to get the job done and right the first time is to help them get there. By providing positive reinforcement when a task is completed successfully, you help to reward good behavior and encourage the continuation of such behavior with similar future tasks or situations. Additionally, coaching when a negative action occurs helps to limit the potential for the same outcome happening again in the future.

Don't be afraid to coach to improve, but make sure that when you help provide feedback it is specific and actionable. What I mean by being specific and actionable is to not go up to a member of your team and simply tell them, "Don't do that again," or, "That was great!" Feedback, both positive and negative, needs to be specific and actionable. What did you like most about what your employee did in a given situation, or what did you not like that they did? How did your employee's actions impact the client?

Think about the situation that occurred and what you would hope for the action to look like in the future. As a leader of a team, not only a manager, you help to empower your team through continual improvement and feedback; this is not learned overnight and will take practice, but know that it is important to not only the success of your franchise or business, but it is also critically important to the success of the individuals that are a part of your team.

By developing an engaged and self-reliable team, you are able to create a foundation where profitability can stem from as we will see with additional ideas on how to create wealth through a franchise model.

Benefits of an Empowered Team

It can be scary seeming to "give up" a certain degree of power to others, but to create a successful foundation within any organization, empowering others is a must. And remember, that you are not "giving up" any power, you are just entrusting it with others with the knowing that they will meet your expectations and provide a positive outcome to the task or assignment. With helping to empower your team and leaders within your franchise or organization, there are multiple benefits that follow that will help both you as a business owner and your business from a profitability standpoint.

One of the first benefits that you will derive from empowerment of others is time. On how many occasions have you asked yourself or wished for "More time in the day?" By empowering others around you and within your organization, you essentially create more time in the day, or at least give yourself the ability to focus on the tasks that are most important as the leader of the business and franchisee. Rather than having to focus on multiple tasks that can be time consuming, the ability to empower others allows you to combine your focus onto the most important items that you have prioritized. With an empowered team within your franchise, associates can help answer baseline questions and solve daily solutions that arise, giving you the ability to focus on strategic planning and analysis for your company to ensure long term success. All too often, business owners and franchisees get caught up in what is known as "Whirlwinds," where the small tasks and miscellaneous items that arise throughout the day throw them off track of where they would have hoped to have been. By empowering the team around you, you help to minimize the miscellaneous "Whirlwinds" and allow you to maintain greater focus on the highest of priorities. Often, these priorities, when focused upon, will lead to grander results for the business which will, in turn, mean increased profitability.

The next key benefit of empowering others within your franchise is Growth. What is your dream for the franchise that you are looking to take part in and develop? Do you see yourself starting one location of the franchise in your local town, or do you see multiple locations developing across several cities? How about multiple locations in multiple states? How about multiple locations of the franchise in multiple countries and growing internationally? Growth in business is at the fundamental nature of what most business owners and franchisees ponder about on a daily basis- how can I make my business grow? With this thought in mind, let me ask you the question that has probably already sprouted in your brain: "How can you grow your business without empowering others?" By empowering others around you and within your organization, you provide the ability to continue to expand your horizons and grow your business effectively. Whether you define growth in your business of acquiring additional clients, or by growing and expanding to multiple locations, empowering others provides the "Water to the seed" in growth.

Growth in business can only be possible when others are entrusted and motivated to provide continual solutions to clients as you, as the franchisee and leader of the organization, have demonstrated and maintained as the expectation. How many of you are there? How many of your team can there be? With this thought in mind, with empowering others, you can begin to think of your team as an extension of yourself as a business leader and franchisee and the individuals that you shape and empower will help to build success in the organization. As much as you may want to, you cannot be in more than one place at the same time; however, the team that you entrust, train, develop, and empower can and will be the face for your franchise at however many locations you are able to establish. With this same idea in mind, as stated previously, it will be critical to maintain a level of expectation and ongoing feedback to positively impact the results and maintain the results that you expect and anticipate as a franchisee.

One of the benefits not commonly grasped immediately by franchisees with the empowerment of others is seeing the benefit in other's development. By empowering others in your team and franchise, whether it be by promoting him or her to a Team Leader position, trainer position, or supervisor, you create development. The benefits surrounding development continue to branch out with enhanced reimbursement within others in the realm of retention within your team, positive service and client outreach, brand recognition, and a multitude of other positive outputs that reflect highly on your organization.

To help get an idea of the benefits found with the empowerment of teams, think back to your first job where you were given a promotion or an additional responsibility such as training new team members. How did it make you feel to be trusted by someone with a higher position? This feeling, the feeling of trust and empowerment, is one that helps build on the thought of success breeding success. As the Chief Executive Officer of Bio-One, I am devoted to helping to develop franchisees and am committed to the success and empowerment of others within their personal franchise locations; this success breeds success and is promoted throughout the organization where franchisees do the same, helping to empower and breed success in others.

Tips on Making Money Through Franchising

Identify your problems, but give your power and energy to solutions. – Tony Robbins

When you first started thinking about the vision of where you want to be in the next year, five years, and beyond what did you dream? Did you dream about being self-sustaining and driving profit margins forward? Most likely. Being able to become a successful franchisee also means being able to make money along the way and maintain a sustainability structure as a franchise. To be able to make money through franchising, there are several guidelines one should follow, and the ability to continue to develop increasing profits through a lengthened timeline with a franchise organization can also become possible with a unique structure that only franchise opportunities allow.

First, as an incoming franchisee, one of the best ways to have the opportunity to make money through franchising is the ability to maintain costs at a low and efficient level, allowing for a quickened pace of reaching a break-even point and profitability. The Bio-One franchise presents a superior example of showing the ability to create profitability and increased money making capability by reduced costs in joining a franchise. Let's take for example that you are considering franchise options, it can be easily attainable that initial franchise costs for a Bio-One Franchise will be less than $75,000 as an initial estimate for franchise startup, whereas a Franchise model such as McDonalds could start anywhere from $900,000 to over $2.3 Million. The ability to gain entrance into a franchise that demonstrates the ability to generate profits allows for a franchisee to make money sooner along the process.

In addition to finding a franchise with reduced entrance fees and costs associated to startup, the ability to create greater profitability through market selection is increased. Franchise options are available throughout the world, creating multiple regional opportunities and unique characteristics that help lead to success or detriment for the business model when placed into the given market. To be able to find a market that has been essentially untapped or underutilized in comparison to the optimal use for a franchise will allow for a franchisee to gain enhanced profitability. This is one of the greatest challenges of most franchise entrances as it is a continual Chess game of finding the next best "move" where a market will take to the advertising and promotional campaigns in such a level that sustains profitability and allows for a greater increase in making money as a franchisee.

After maintaining efficiencies in a franchise model and finding a location that is most suitable to creating success, the next idea in helping to create profits as a part of the franchise model is continual expansion and multiple locations. As a franchisee, one of your primary goals will be to create a self-driven team where you feel comfortable with delegating the full range of tasks that require business production to run smoothly and in a high quality manner. By being able to shape and mold an efficient team around you as a franchisee, you will also develop the potential of being able to copy the franchise model to other locations and continue to impact additional markets. Several Bio-One Franchisees have had the ability to create sustainable success and enhanced profitability through the development of multiple franchise markets with the organization. By being able to become a more effective franchisee and leader within the organization at Bio-One, you gain the additional ability to make more money at a greater rate.

Essentially, it becomes easier to replicate the business model after creating the success in one market. As a franchisee at Bio-One, you gain access to valuable tools and experiences that will make you a top business leader in the industry, allowing you to gain valuable insight as how to succeed in multiple areas with proficient delegation. The continual building of multiple franchise locations and markets will create even more success and profits than you may have originally anticipated and will also create for a decrease in market-based risk as having a presence in multiple locations can help to ward off profitability swings based on changes in demand.

The opportunity to earn money through franchising is out there, and by partnering with Bio-One as a franchisee, you are able to develop profits at a quickened pace in comparison to other franchise models available throughout the world today.

Cost Analysis Strategies

A business has to be involving, it has to be fun, and it has to exercise your creative instincts.

— Richard Branson

By this point, you have clearly identified your top options for a potential franchise and are beginning to look more and more closely at the final decision as to where you are looking to attribute your time and energy in the upcoming future to yield a desired set of results. It is my hope that you will find that Bio-One helps to meet the qualifications and set of criteria that you have developed within your search, but I realize that this type of business is not for everyone. Even if you decide that your criteria is not a match for Bio-One, I want to be able to give you key takeaways that you can apply to your overall search and application from today and into the future as business continues. The next tool to add to your "franchise tool box" is that of cost analysis strategies.

To get an idea of the importance of cost analysis strategies, let's look at the importance of cost analysis that economists and business leaders have placed on the ideal over the course of time. If you were to sit down in an Economics course today in any country throughout the world, you will come away with two primary rules that will be ingrained and taught day after day: first, there is no such thing as a "free lunch," and second, "when supply equals demand, everything is golden." We will get to supply equaling demand later, but the first fundamental that we are focusing on this section is that of, "no such thing as a free lunch."

Never Such Thing as a Free Lunch

At the foundation of developing cost analysis strategies when comparing available franchise options to pursue, or after a franchise has been chosen and you are looking to make a strategic decision as a franchisee, there will be opportunity cost involved. Above the costs that are attributed due to inventory, labor, or overhead, there is another cost that is often unrealized at first, but plays a dramatic impact on the long term results of the organization- the opportunity cost. The opportunity cost, or the cost of the option that is given up or not pursued, is a cost that is weighed and attributed after every decision that is made by a franchisee, or franchisee candidate. By deciding to go with one franchise over another, you have an opportunity cost in that there is some level of potential value that may be given up to follow through on the decision being made. Just as you are doing now by creating a checklist of personal priorities and expectations, the similar thought process should be continued into future decisions that are made to help ensure that there is minimal impact to opportunity cost.When making important decisions as a potential franchisee, or when you are immersed as a veteran franchisee in the future, weigh the options available to you and think about what the potential outcomes would be for either decision being made to help gain a perspective on what your true cost will be. And also, remember that the next time that someone asks you to meet up for a "free lunch," think about what else you could be doing with that time- that is your opportunity cost.

Cost Benefit Analysis Process

Continuing from the idea of opportunity cost, let's now take a closer look at a systematic approach to cost-benefit analysis that can help you to quantify available options as a potential franchisee. The cost-benefit analysis, also referred to as CBA, has been identified as being a way for business owners and franchisees to estimate and review potential strengths and weaknesses for a given set of options available. Cost-benefit analysis strategy can be implanted to cost savings measures, labor and hiring decisions, procedure implementation, vendor decisions, and just about anything else that you can think of that will imply some type of cost or impact to the business model. There will never be a 100 percent certain way to compare all benefits and potential outcomes involved based on decisions made within a business or organization, but cost-benefit analysis will most likely yield the most accurate and reliable information to help make educated and impactful decisions.

By effectively developing a cost-benefit analysis, a franchisee and leader within an organization can begin to understand if a given decision will be a sound investment for the future of the business, or can be seen as justifiable based on the measure of risk versus reward. Additionally, the implementation of cost-benefit analysis, as you are doing now in weighing the decision between available options, helps to gain an idea of what the overall total costs will be for individual options and made easier to compare between benefits available. This is where we want to look further with implementation in your decision to be a franchisee as well as a solid framework for the franchise "tool belt" that you are developing for future needs.

As a franchisee, or franchisee candidate, your mind will most likely be focused on the bottom-line results- how will this decision impact the profitability of my business? Cost-benefit analysis provides a monetary breakdown of compared benefits, helping to correlate directly to the bottom-line focus that you have as a franchisee.

Within cost-benefit analysis, you will follow a formulated process to begin comparing available options. First, identify what available alternative options, programs, or activities are available in alignment with the main goal that you have. Second, take into account and list all individuals and organizations that will be impacted by the decision that will be made. For example, will the decision impact your family or your employee's families, will this decision impact the relationship that you have maintained with a vendor, or will this decision make a dramatic impact into the community in which you are a part of? There are many stakeholders involved with each decision, and they should be thought of and put into the analysis that you are undertaking with the cost-benefit approach.

The next items that you want to begin to develop in regard to cost-benefit analysis is working to identify how you will measure the impact of the decision being made and at what time period; a long-term activity or decision will most likely have a higher cost impact as compared to a short-term activity. With making the decision between franchise options, for example, this decision will relate to long-term costs and benefits and would be weighted for that timeframe, whereas other decisions, such as to commit to a 3-month billboard advertisement, would be a much shorter impact duration.

After combining stakeholder information, cost with time-frame data, and predicted benefit information, you want to calculate to the best estimation possible as to what the overall monetary cost will be for each option in relation to benefits anticipated. By conducting the procedural analysis, you will be able to clearly identify differences in cost for available options and make a resolution that is most justifiable and advantageous.

To help provide a visual representation of cost-benefit analysis per available option, use the following equation as a guide to your decision making process:

Estimate of Benefits – (Current Costs + Future Costs + Opportunity Cost) = Net Value of Decision

Reward Yourself Through Franchise Development

In the business world, everyone is paid in two coins: cash and experience. Take the experience first; the cash will come later. – Harold Geneen

By continuing to develop a franchise, whether it be at Bio-One or any number of additional franchise options available to you as a franchisee candidate, you are able to be rewarded at multiple levels along the way. First and foremost, franchisees are most often rewarded with bottom line profitability and sales performance.

By driving profits and maintaining efficiencies through the business model, a franchisee is able to realize profits and be rewarded through the development of the organization that they build upon each and every day. Being able to reward yourself with peace of mind by creating a nest egg for the future and creating sustainable personal finances is an incredible benefit of being a franchisee that is often realized in a much more delayed fashion, if even not at all, if you were to stay in the corporate world where your fate is often not in your own hands. Being rewarded through franchise development spans far beyond the bottom line performance of an organization and goes much deeper into the personal side of business.

Being a franchisee requires the development of multiple ranges of skill sets, from being an industry leading expert to enhanced relationship building experiences that will also help to illustrate a rewarding environment for development. A franchisee is presented with opportunities each and every day that stretch their imaginations and build skill sets that will be overarching for the remainder of their careers. By continually being faced with the need to maximize relationships with clients, vendors, and team members, factors such as communication and negotiating are emphasized and given the opportunity to become more efficient.

As a franchisee you will be rewarded every day, especially with Bio-One. Every opportunity that pushes you beyond your limits and creates the need to think critically and expand upon skill sets will be a consideration of being rewarded in the present moment and into the future as a leader with the organization as well as any additional future organizations you are a part of for years to come.

Community-Based Partnerships for Success

Business is more exciting than any game.
– Lord Beaverbrook

Being able to strengthen relationships within a community is a vital piece of maintaining success within an organization and being able to establish a foundation of success at the beginning stages is at the root of these relationships. At Bio-One, creating relationships within the community has been a critical element of being able to maintain the 100 percent success model that we emphasize. By realizing at an early stage how important relationships, not only within your own business model and organization, but within the community that you participate and transact business, you will be able to create higher levels of success at a much more efficient rate than that of organizations that look past the community and see it only as a means for creating sales or profits. The factor of engaging within the community is yet another example of "Helping first, business second."

Examples of Community Partnerships

Chamber of Commerce

There are countless community partnerships and resources that provide support to incoming organizations and should be considered as a part of action planning toward success measures. One of the first places to start with a startup business or franchise is with the local Chamber of Commerce as a place to look for influential community partnerships, as most Chambers have the general mission to help enhance economic growth within the region they are established, help to provide education to business leaders, and help to promote organizations in connection with the Chamber of Commerce. Additionally, by combining together many business leaders from a geographical area, a Chamber of Commerce works to strengthen local economies, creates key networking opportunities that are valuable to gain additional personable relationships, and also help to represent the interest of local businesses with government and regulations being established.

By becoming a member of your local Chamber of Commerce through a franchise, you will also receive additional benefits that become highly advantageous when creating effective marketing campaigns and in working to develop brand recognition within the community you operate. A Chamber of Commerce provides a standard of recognition throughout the year at various events as well as actual membership identification materials or emblems that can be used as a part of marketing materials, or even displayed in the physical business location. Additional marketing material and promotions are commonly associated with Chambers of Commerce around the United States in relation to business events in the community, ribbon cuttings, Business After Hours events, social networking opportunities, and email listserves that each work to help to develop the brand and recognition of businesses a part of the local chamber.

Along the same lines of providing networking opportunities for business leaders, a Chamber of Commerce can also promote referral opportunities between the members to help engage different partners within the Chamber. By leveraging these one-on-one relationships as a business leader and franchisee, you can become better connected within the local community and uncover untapped opportunities for the continuation of business.

The benefit of providing education and consulting opportunities to Chamber members is another aspect that is constructive for incoming franchisees looking to gain unique perspectives and experience on conducting business in the community. By gaining information presented by knowledgeable business leaders that have learned, first hand, what it takes to succeed in a very specific community setting, there will usually be highly beneficial information that can be relatable to your own actions and plans in sustaining success, both now and into the future.

Contact your local Chamber of Commerce as you head into business leadership and see how they can assist in all stages of business development.

Better Business Bureau

Developing a level of trust between a franchise and the local community is important when starting out within a community, especially if the franchise has not been known by name in the past, or if there has been minimal brand development up to this point. To help gain trust from many individuals within the community, the Better Business Bureau can be a great resource. The Better Business Bureau has been an established organization and resource for businesses in the United States for over 100 years, and even extends internationally. Often referred to as the BBB, the Better Business Bureau helps to provide trustworthy ratings and information from an outside perspective, allowing individuals to make decisions as to which organization to conduct business with based on these ratings.

In addition to providing third-party ratings, the Better Business Bureau is an organization that receives and uncovers complaints as well as recognition of businesses in a community. This factor is important to consider as a franchisee as the information shared with the BBB could potentially have negative impacts if not monitored. As a community resource, the BBB should be consistently monitored by franchisees to quickly control any potential negative information being relayed to potential consumers within the community. If a complaint is raised, the situation should be immediately responded to and resolved by the best of your ability as a franchisee and work to correct any bottom-line issues that may have caused the complaint to be raised.

With positive ratings and feedback shared through the Better Business Bureau, a franchisee can also use this information to help support brand development and marketing implementation. Positive reviews and ratings can be published on social media, in company newsletters, and can even be positioned on windows or on countertops at physical business locations. Each opportunity to help share positive ratings attributed by the Better Business Bureau will help a franchise to create valuable trust-based relationships within the community that they are a part of.

Kiwanis, Rotary, Lions, etc.

The organizations that often meet for lunchtime meetings on Tuesdays or Thursdays at the local restaurant and help to support initiatives in the community can be a platform for networking as a franchisee. As the CEO of Bio-One, I continually look for opportunities to connect our franchisees with additional leaders in the communities that we participate in as an organization, and benefactor clubs such as Kiwanis, Rotary and Lions are historically-based opportunities to leverage connections. The connections that are built through these organizations add to the level of established personal relationships among peer leaders in the community.

In addition to helping provide support amongst one another as business leaders through community organizations such as Kiwanis, Rotary, or Lions club, the factor of giving back to the community through compassionate and charitable efforts helps to enrich the lives of others in the community. As Bio-One continually emphasizes "help first, business second," giving back to the community is always top of mind and these organizations help to support that mission.

Non-Profit Boards or Foundations

Continuing with the mindset and goal of helping to give back to the community, I encourage franchisees through Bio-One, and really any business leader, to look for connections within their communities to give back their time and experience to help non-profit organizations by serving on a board of directors. As we have previously established, as a franchisee candidate, you possess a great wealth of knowledge and experience that helps to put you in the successful position and opportunity that you are in. These skills can continue to be enhanced, developed, and toned through the participation in non profits and the skills can, likewise, be transitioned to help with the vision of other organizations.

As a franchisee, it is important to be able to continue to expand your development as a leader and strategic planner, and working with a nonprofit organization greatly helps with this need. Nonprofit organizations often need guidance with brand development, fundraising, communication strategies, and many other directly-transferable requirements that help to build a successful franchise. At Bio-One, franchisees are encouraged to become engaged with additional organizations that they feel passionately about, ranging from the arts to *Habitat for Humanity*.

In addition to the community partnerships, at Bio-One, we continue to work hand in hand with law enforcement, fire officials, first responders, coroner offices, housing associations and numerous additional resources to help create sustainable success. One must be able to realize the importance of maximizing relationships within a community and marketplace in order to drive profitability forward. By placing a high emphasis on this full range of relationships in each of the communities that we are a part of at Bio-One, we create the ability to get firsthand awareness of available new jobs that come into view and create the ability to profit, while also helping the community as a whole and providing a unique resource through the services that we provide that also help to elevate the performance of each external organization partnered with.

The connections built among the board of directors within these organizations will play critical roles in long-term success for the franchise and franchisee. In the sense of becoming connected with nonprofit boards of directors, franchisees focus on helping people, helping the community, and helping their own business model with critical levels of development.

The Right Mindset
for Franchising

The mindset that you are in right now- what is it? How are you feeling about becoming a franchisee? I want to dive deeper into the mindset that you have currently and how you can leverage the strengths and opportunities in your own personal characteristics and mindset to develop continual success in the franchise that you pursue. Having a strong mind with the ability to continually learn and take on new challenges is one of the first steps to realizing that you will be successful in your future franchise endeavors, but there is much more. In the following sections, we will take a look at some of the personality and entrepreneurial traits that help some standout among the crowd, identifying the most successful franchisees and helping to identify the strengths that you can personally bring to the table.

Personality Types for Success in Franchising

As one begins to think about the opportunity of moving into a franchise and taking on the task of being an entrepreneur, there are several characteristics that will help to determine the overall success that one will have in their pursuits, no matter the franchise they decide to embark on. There are a full range of challenges and opportunities that will be faced during the journey of franchising and the following characteristics help one to visualize the ability of a franchisee to handle the multitude of situations present and the potential stress-factors involved. Let's take a look at some of the top characteristics that help to identify a successful franchisee.

Risk Aversion

The idea that owning a business or becoming a franchisee is a consideration of a gamble, or the idea that it takes an individual that is apt to take on risk, is far from the truth behind a successful franchisee. In actuality, an individual pursuing a franchise should have a level of risk aversion in that they will be willing to take on some degree of risk but at a controlled rate that is small and calculated.

All business entities, whether it be an established corporation for 50 years, a start-up, or a franchise, has an involvement of risk of failure, but there is something that sets franchise business models apart- proven track record. A strong franchise that has created a proven track record of success helps to minimize risk involved with business development and helps individuals to evaluate the level of risk involved with specific franchise opportunities. A risk assessment can be completed both internally (mind set of individual) and externally (level of risk present with a given franchise) by a potential franchisee before making the decision to invest in their future with or without the given franchise.

Keeping With What Works

As an individual looking to take part in something new or different as a part of becoming a franchisee and you are concerned about the fact that you may not have an inner entrepreneurial drive that says, "Change things up to succeed," you are in the right place. All too often, entrepreneurs feel as though the wheel must constantly be reinvented in order to succeed, and many times they may also have an uncontrollable urge to reinvent processes or entire organizations in order to obtain maximum results; however, when it comes to becoming a successful franchisee, this is simply not true.

A successful franchisee, rather than try to reinvent the wheel, should seek a proven system that has identified a roadmap for success. A franchisee does not have to take the time to figure out a new or different way to find the best process for doing something in that there has already been a framework and system of operation developed that will give an outline of the best way to do something in order to achieve desired results within the business. This is not to say that an inner drive and determination to help make things better is not good or necessary, it just helps to illustrate that, with franchising, not everything has to be reinvented to be successful. Additionally, an individual looking to pursue franchising has the ability to take this inner drive and entrepreneurial spirit to help learn through processes and avoid mistakes, helping to make the transition into a new franchise endeavor more successful at a faster rate.

Let's take a look at the "Build a Bike" example:

How Do You Build a Bike?

Think to yourself for a moment about the process of building a bike or putting together a bike for your child's birthday. After you come home from the store, you open the bike box and find one hundred separate parts and pieces that have been designed to fit together and provide movement and fluidity to the bike, allowing your child to safely go from one point to another on two wheels. Within the bike box, and among the hundred or more so parts, there is a set of instructions that helps to outline every step that is needed in order to bring all of the separate pieces together and create a working bicycle that can then be enjoyed. At this point, you have a decision to make- are you going to follow the instructions that have been laid out in front of you or are you going to go with the train of thought that instructions should only be used if "all else fails?" The decision is yours- what would you decide?

Much like the process of building a bike or putting together furniture from IKEA, for example, that requires the need to follow a set of instructions in order to have a successful conclusion, the same process is demonstrated with that of a franchise. At the core fundamentals of starting a franchise and becoming an investor within an idea that will carry one forward, there is a set of instructions that are designed to pave the way to success. When thinking about the potential of starting a franchise, one of the initial questions that you want to ask yourself is: "Will I be able to follow instructions put in front of me to be successful?" If your answer is yes, then continue with the investment, if your answer is no, then there might be a few areas to consider.

Building a business from the ground up can feel like a whirlwind of information and options colliding in one space known as "entrepreneurship," but starting a business from the framework of a franchise provides the opportunity to have a set of "instructions." As a franchisee, one receives access to tools and resources and instructions as how to be marketable, operationally sound, and a multitude of other critical elements that have essentially been proven in the past to create a successful outcome. By being able to follow these instructions that are laid out before you as a franchisee, you can become successful. It's not to say that you will not be able to incorporate new energy and ideas to help continue to better the business model or make adjustments to the specific market that you are operating in, but the framework has been designated.

Going back to the idea of building a bike from the ground up- think of the marketing direction as the gears of the bike that can adjust depending on the terrain and incline to help propel the business forward; think of the finance direction as the handle bars of the bike, as those must be placed on straight and in solidity to ensure the bike goes in the correct direction at all times; think of the operational direction of the franchise as the wheels and spokes of the bike, as they operate in smooth rhythm to help move the bike and individual forward and in the direction that has been guided by other processes. If one piece of the bike is incorrectly put together or forgotten, the ability to maintain a safe bike ride and reach the desired destination will not be possible. Think to yourself, "Can I follow a set of directions to succeed?" If yes, continue, if no, think about the bike.

Coachability

> **Continuous learning is the minimum requirement for success in any field.**
> – Dennis Waitley

Learn something new every day. The ability to consistently learn from others and adapt to opportunities that arise within a franchise is at the base foundation for success found with a franchisee. As a successful franchisee, one has to be able to ask for help and guidance when in doubt and should not be hesitant to contact the franchisor for support. Additionally, the ability to gain insight from other business models, business leaders, and franchises adds to the level of coachability and continual learning that identifies the opportunity to succeed. Advice and knowledge only gets someone so far; in order to be successful, a franchisee must act upon the knowledge obtained and follow advice given. A franchisee or even a seasoned business leader or Chief Executive Officer of a multinational corporation will never have all of the answers, but the ability to seek advice and ask for help when needed while having an open mind to continual learning will help pave the way for success.

Diligence

Sometimes, and often times, a franchisee will have to roll up their sleeves and work hard to achieve success. Essentially, a franchisee must have the willingness and aptitude to do whatever it takes to get the job done, because at the end of the day it will come back to what is "put into it." The attitude of diligence is demonstrated in every action of a franchisee- from leading by example with putting in longer hours, to handling multiple tasks at one time, to helping clean the restrooms and countertops- hard work is demonstrated in all actions. No matter the type of business or organization that one is looking to join as a part of a franchise or other business model, it takes hard work to be successful, but more than "hard work," it is "Smart" work. A franchisee can work smarter through the business model developed and have efficiencies maintained in order to create success. One looking to succeed in franchising should be able to know and immediately accept the fact that it will take diligence to reach their ideal of success, and always remember that the harder they work, as a leader, the harder their teams and support staff around them will work to help achieve results. Success in franchising is where hard work meets opportunity.

At Bio-One, diligence is a must-have quality, where every franchisee is required to roll up their sleeves and get in the trenches just like anyone else. As the founder of Bio-One, I myself am no stranger to what it takes to get the job done when cleaning up sites that have been part of a tragedy or horrific situation. From hoarding situations to homicide cleanups, Bio-One franchisees know what it takes to be successful when it comes to demonstrating diligence within the position. Another way to think about diligence in Bio-One is "sweat equity" where drops of sweat on a job site bring about profitability and brand development into the future, all completed without ever re-victimizing a victim.

People First

To be successful, you have to have your heart in your business, and your business in your heart.

– Sr. Thomas Watson

The ability to interact with people is at the core of every business- without people, there is no business. A successful franchisee will be one that has proven interpersonal skills and has the ability to effectively manage relationships and interact with employees, vendors, and customers in a way that promotes positive business performance. The interpersonal skills present by a franchisee will help to create impactful loyalty, trust and value within the organization and within the community to develop the opportunity to succeed.

As stated, Bio-One lives up to the ideals of "Help first, business second" in each realm of the business model; from myself as Chief Executive Officer, to the newest addition to the staff, every individual works to represent the mentality of meeting the needs of people, then focusing on the business benefit. By relating to clients and people, the business aspect will come- great sales do not create great service- great service is what creates great sales.

Entrepreneurial Traits for Success

❝I'm convinced that about half of what separates the successful entrepreneurs from the non-successful ones is pure perseverance.❞ – Steve Jobs

Similar to the section previously, where we took a closer look at some of the traits that help to identify successful franchisees, I wanted to take a moment and continue to look at additional traits that entrepreneurs and franchisees share in success. One of the fundamental ideas and realities that I have come to know over my experience with Bio-One and in the franchise industry as a whole is that no leader or business owner has the same strengths and qualities as the next; each leader and franchisee within bio one has a unique set of qualities that helps to make them who they are. In this section I want to outline some of the characteristics of entrepreneurs and business leaders that I have seen work well within franchising and feel that it will be helpful in your journey to deciding as to where you are headed with a potential franchise.

Business Focus

In the world of business, whether it is in franchising or other-wise, focus must be maintained to create a pathway to success. Even outside the world of business, focus is incredibly important in order to create successful outcomes for personal endeavors. A great example of how focus creates the ability to sustain positive performance and leads to successful outcomes is seen through the visualization and focus process that Olympic and Endurance Athletes, such as an Ironman triathlete, maintain in their respective competition. 140.6 miles, consisting of a 2.4 mile swim, 112 mile bike ride, and 26.2 run are only successfully completed when an athlete maintains upmost focus and visualization of success. Before an Ironman athlete ever hits the water to start the ultimate triathlon challenge, they visualize themselves at the finish line and visualize every moment of what must be conquered in order to be called an "Ironman" within the next 17 hours of their competition, taking into account the strategy to undertake in nutrition and form in each of the three disciplines.

Similar to how an Ironman triathlete visualizes success at the finish line, a franchisee and entrepreneur must be able to maintain the same level of focus to cross the metaphorical finish line of success at every turn, especially when thinking of a long term success plan for the business. By visualizing how a business will run and engage within the community helps to provide focus for business owners and allows for the ability to think through potential hurdles that may be faced along the way. Even the most successful franchisees continue to dream and visualize about how their respective business projects and deals created will build into the future and what the next day, month, or year will bring. By bringing an element of focus to each activity pursued, a franchisee becomes more effective in each action and can make a conscious effort to meet the deadline established.

Creativity

When coming into the world of franchising, many franchisee candidates often think that there is no room for creativity in the business that they are investing within, concerned to stay within the lines that have been drawn before them.

As the Chief Executive Officer of the Bio-One franchise, where we are recognized by having a 100 percent success rate, I feel that creativity and having a franchisee as a creative thinker is essential. A creative thinker, when in the position of a franchisee, is able to think beyond boundaries, explore additional options to help solve problems, generate new ideas for marketing and branding within unique regions and markets, and is able to engage with diverse teams and clients with the ability to have varying perspective. Additionally, by being able to think beyond the box, creative thinking franchisees are also able to develop the mindset that there is not a box when it comes to defining success within the organization. By expanding horizons of success and being able to adapt in unique situations, I look to creative thinking and overall creativity as a positive in developing top franchisees. Don't be afraid to enhance your creativity and bring it to the table when developing your marketing plan and engagement techniques.

Ethics

Have you ever come across the poster or saying that states, "Everything you ever need to know, you learned in kindergarten?" It often seems simple, and all too often overlooked, but the quality of honesty and ethics in business practices is something that every successful leader should develop and maintain within their organization. Honesty is a direct reflection of the level of ethics that you personally hold to yourself when no one else is looking and becomes more important when reflected upon a team that you are responsible for and leading on a daily basis.

A good way to think about ethics when it comes to becoming a franchisee is thinking about potential situations where your ethical balance and honesty may be tested; this is where the idea of "Help first, and business second" becomes emphasized once again. There are countless situations, whether it be with vendors, employees, or clients, where honesty and ethical practices may be tested and will require you to make a decision as a leader within the organization that can have either positive or negative influence.

To help think with high morality in ethical-based situations that will most certainly arise in any franchise or business model, the practice that I use is what is commonly referred to as the "Headline Approach" to ethics. The Headline Approach as a franchisee is where you think about how a given situation and decision could be perceived by the general public if posted on the nightly news or daily paper as a headline. Let's take for example that you are making the decision of going with a given set of vendors for a supplementary service for your business, you weigh the options between two primary vendors and are ready to make a final decision. Before making the final decision, you uncover information that one of the vendors, although providing a lower price as compared to the competitor, has been recently cited for several violations in relation to environmental hazards. If you were to choose to conduct business with the lower-priced vendor, you may end up in an ethical dilemma where a potential headline could read, "ABC Franchise Takes Lower Cost over Helping the Environment," whereas if you were to choose the slightly higher-priced vendor that has been recognized for environmentally friendly practices, the headline may read, "ABC Franchise Looks to Help the Environment while Helping Clients." This is a thought process that may help you to make ethically-based decisions with positive outcomes in mind.

Most decisions made with an ethical basis will never make it into the headlines, but each decision that you make as a leader within your organization is mirrored to your employees and is reflected upon the clients that you serve. By leading with high ethical standards, you will be able to positively influence and encourage your team to uphold the same standards and, in addition to a friendlier environment, you will also have the ability to maintain higher profitability within the business model by retaining clients. Keep honesty in mind and remember the valuable tools that you learned in Kindergarten in order to succeed as a franchisee.

Communicate Effectively

"To effectively communicate, we must realize that we are all different in the way we perceive the world and use this understanding as a guide to our communication with others." – Tony Robbins

---

Not much work can be completed if you don't learn to communicate effectively across work teams, within vendor relationships, and with clients served. Often, you may have the perfect idea of what you are looking to accomplish in your head and have envisioned what success will look like, but if you are unable to clearly communicate the goals and vision to others, the results will never be achieved. If you have had minimal experience with communicating with others in team environments or in a business setting, or feel uncomfortable with speaking in front of groups or in one-on-one situations, I highly suggest that you begin focusing and practicing on these skills immediately. By being able to clearly and confidently express what you need done within a business is at the base of being able to realize goals envisioned.

The fear of public speaking and communication ranks among the highest fears by individuals throughout the world, often coming in higher than the fear of death, so it is understandable if you may feel uneasy about communicating at first with others or in a group setting. But as said before, if you feel that your communication skills and comfort level needs to be perfected or honed, I recommend practicing immediately. One of the best ways to get better at communicating and speaking in front of groups is to put yourself into situations where skills are tested and practiced.

Practicing communication skills can be as simple as having a discussion at your favorite coffee shop with a complete stranger or with the Barista making your favorite blend of coffee. By expanding your comfort level with speaking one-on-one in situations where you may not have normally conducted a conversation will allow you to build on critical skills that can then be applied to coaching conversations or rapport building with clients within your business. There are organizations in many communities throughout the United States and throughout the World that also provide public speaking opportunities and practice such as your local Chamber of Commerce, *Toast Masters*, Rotary, Kiwanis, or your local Small Business Development Center or even public library. Think about any current organizations that you volunteer or coach with, or maybe even your kids participate in that will allow you to build your communication skills.

Another great place to build communication skills is with your spouse or roommate at home. The "negotiating" conversations completed between spouses over weekly chores or "Honey-Do's" can actually be applied to communication activities observed and conducted within a franchise setting. So, the next time that you have an argument with your spouse and are working to resolve the given situation, think about the communication skills you evoke and how those can be applied to resolving a potential conflict-based situation with a client or employee.

The application of communication within the franchise setting continues on multiple levels and is observed on a daily basis in any type of business model throughout the world. As the franchisee and leader for your business, it is going to be critical to help train new team members and help to enhance a work environment that is productive. In order to create this atmosphere, effective communication must be in place, and this starts with you. Having a positive and healthy communication relationship with your team is created by developing consistent information and conversations with those around you. It can be as simple as having an open-door policy and working alongside your team, or ensuring that you make it a top priority to talk with each member of your staff on a daily basis and have daily huddle sessions where you communicate business happenings. By creating an open and welcoming environment through communication and by maintaining consistent communication channels and delivery of pertinent information, you help to enhance the level of trust that your team and others have with you and will be directly reflected in the effort that they put into their work.

The difference from being a leader rather than a manager often stems from communication. Just as it is important to build rapport and enhance relationships with clients, it is even that much more important to do the same with your team. Communication in a positive and friendly manner allows you to encourage personal discussion with your team and helps to build morale that is positively reflected in results achieved by any franchise. As a leader, you work to create a productive environment that is one in which team members look forward to being a part of, rather than dreading on their way into work. This environment becomes possible when positive communication channels and reinforcement through communication become a daily habit.

Again, if you are not comfortable in a given scenario that causes you to lean on communication skills, put yourself into a position now that will push you beyond your comfort zone and will help to create the all-important skills of communication, otherwise, how are you going to be able to communicate the incredible results you are going to achieve with your franchise?

Confidence

Business requires confidence to perform at a highly sustained level. When times are good and when times are slow, confidence is needed as a franchisee to maintain a mindset that allows for quick and steadfast decision making. Confidence will be important in the first months and year of a franchise being established where there may be moments that are worrying or that did not go according to your plan, and your confidence will be tested to avoid any anxiety felt by the team or vendors. As a franchisee and leader within your business, you will be responsible for not only maintaining team morale and working to minimize problem situations when they arise, but you will be called upon to display a level of confidence that will become identified as the "face" of the business and organization. By maintaining an adequate and steady level of confidence, you will also help to build your team's confidence in similarly challenging situations that they may face. As the leader of the franchise, you will be looked upon for a model of confidence, making it that much more important to demonstrate a calm demeanor when challenging situations are faced. Confidence as a franchisee will help you to make the tough decisions when needed and will help to ensure that your team around you continues to move forward through the ups and downs that are faced by business trend in any industry.

Positivity

Similar to maintaining confidence as a leader and franchisee, positivity and displaying a positive attitude are also elemental traits that successful individuals portray in the franchise world. As one that will be motivating a team to achieve goals within a franchise, maintaining a positive attitude will help to keep high energy levels and keep the team moving toward successful outcomes. Sharing in positivity and developing positive attitudes in others as a part of a team can be as simple as providing some snacks in the office every now and then or helping to provide one-on-one advice or recognition when positive actions or results are achieved.

At Bio-One, we consistently work to provide a franchise atmosphere that is more similar to a family than a work environment. By building upon the idea that we can work hard and play hard, we are able to maintain the fine balance between productivity and liveliness that is important for many franchise models that put team members in challenging situations. By maintaining positive environments and work flow between franchisees and team members at Bio-One, we help to create an atmosphere where team members will not hesitate to lend an extra hand or stick around for a longer shift, always helping to devote the highest quality of work possible, to help support and build upon the brand of Bio-One while positively impacting the bottom line performance. Think positive, act positive, and be positive and positive results will emerge as you take on the reigns of being a franchisee.

Inspirational

❝The mediocre teacher tells. The good teacher explains. The superior teacher demonstrates. The great teacher inspires.❞– William Arthur Ward

Some qualities that are sought after by franchisees and business leaders from around the globe are not able to be taught, they are intangible. One of the qualities that I look for in myself and in others that I work with as a part of Bio-One, is the quality of being inspirational and working to inspire others. Think for a moment about what inspires you? Is it your family? Your young child, perhaps, talking and walking for the first time? Maybe something that inspires you is not an individual at all, but something in nature, such as watching the sunset fall below the horizon. The idea of being inspirational and being able to inspire your team to achieve results can sometimes be hard to imagine, but it is possible to achieve, and I feel that everyone has the potential to inspire, they just have to make the decision to do so.

At the fundamental grass roots of inspiring others in a business, it is simply looking forward and sharing in a vision of what the future will hold. In the beginning of a franchise, it can sometimes seem daunting for a franchisee and new employees and it may be hard for them to initially see the vision that you have in mind, but being able to inspire through forecasting and a clear illustration of what that future will look like, for themselves and the business, will work together to achieve positive results.

By helping to make your team invested within the organization and feeling a level of connection to accomplishments made, inspiration is found. Additionally, by helping to generate enthusiasm around large projects and goals made, or gathering input from a team to set short-term and long-term goals, inspiration can be developed with showing the benefits of the hard work being put in.

A simple "thank you" can go a long way and remembering to acknowledge your team for a job well done when the work is hard can help to show the team that you care, and likewise, will create inspiration. As a franchisee, you can also ask your team directly as to what inspires them and motivates them to come to work every day. Build upon what drives your team, individually, and create development plans geared toward these goals established; by showing your team that you are vested in their development and personal growth, this will also help to yield the feeling of inspiration.

Even though inspiration and being inspiring toward others can often be thought of as intangible, there are several activities, as shown above, that you can do with your teams once you take part in the franchise to help build positive results. Acknowledge the hard work that has been completed, commend team members for their efforts, be vested in others development, and keep focus toward what the future will bring to help create inspiration within your organization that you embark.

Drive and Determination

❝Start where you are. Use what you have. Do what you can.❞ – Arthur Ashe

Another quality that I look for in successful franchisees is another intangible set of qualities known as drive and determination. Going into business for yourself or within a franchise has helped to identify that you already have that inner drive to not accept the status quo and push beyond the mediocre. Drive and determination are qualities that very few individuals have, where many become satisfied with a given position within their organization or life. But others, such as yourself, see something different of them and want to seek a higher success rate than the status quo that others have "worked" to create. By having this inner drive, you have made the conscious decision to look for an opportunity that will push you past mediocre and into a greater level of success through pursuing a franchise and being your own boss. This drive that you maintain will be essential to creating sustained success into the future and will need to be harnessed as trends evolve over time.

In addition to inner-drive, the determination factor is the next ingredient that will help to separate you from those that may quit when times become challenging. Determination is another un-teachable characteristic that helps to identify a truly successful individual and is something that I look for in Bio-One Franchisees. If a franchisee is faced with a daunting task ahead in a crime cleanup or situation that may be unsuitable to those with a weak stomach, we need someone that will have the determination to get the job done no matter what is faced. The determination factor will help franchisees to be able to maintain the positive mindset that is needed during these challenging situations to keep positive with clients and help to ensure that individuals are never re-victimized when facing a challenging situation. It is the challenging situations that bring out the best in determination and these situations are what we face every day at Bio-One.

Think you are ready for the challenge? Again, by diving into this book and searching further into the process of becoming a franchisee, you have already demonstrated the value of determination and this is a quality that will continue to pay dividends as you move further in the process, leveraging strengths and opportunities in the business model undertaken.

How to Think and Act Like a Fortune 500 Franchise

From the smallest of startup businesses and organizations, founded in local communities and often referred to as the "Mom and Pop Shops" of the past, to the largest multinational organizations that span continents and cultures, there are integrated fundamentals that stay consistent among all organizations. To become a successful franchisee, and to really be a fundamentally supportive and integrated business leader within any organization, it is critical to maintain a mindset that is broad encompassing and reflects the actions of a Fortune 500 company. By emulating some of the world's foremost leaders and movers, a franchisee can become successful themselves and help to run a business that is at the head of the competition. There are multiple levels of expertise and business integration that can be applied to any business structure and it is within these applications that we want to work to determine what will be most attributable to your personal success.

Let's evaluate these applications one at a time.

SWOT Analysis

At the fundamental baseline of any organization, the ability to analyze and perceive internal and external factors that impact the ability to succeed are considered to be of utmost importance. Using a SWOT analysis (a process that identifies the strengths, weaknesses, opportunities and threats of an organisation), an individual, such as a franchisee candidate can also look at an organization from an external standpoint and determine factors that may continue to impact the franchise's ability to succeed into the future, given the amount of impact that each related factor may have in comparison to the organization. A SWOT Analysis creates a visual and organized manner for a franchisee candidate or business leader to begin the analysis process of an organization that they are looking to invest within.

Looking closer at the SWOT Analysis method of evaluating an organization, we will begin to breakdown the critical components of Strengths, Weaknesses, Opportunities and Threats (SWOT) that a business or organization is faced with when working to develop success within a given industry.

Strengths

"Tell me about what you are most good at." Strengths of an organization are the factors and processes held within a franchise that are identified as the strongest points that work with the other components of the organization to create successful outcomes. Strengths are important to understand as a part of an organization from an analysis standpoint as this understanding will help a franchisee or business leader to make key decisions that leverage these strengths to overcome additional obstacles sure to be faced into the future.

Strengths, when comparing franchise options as a candidate, should be looked at in perspective of competitors within the industry. Several questions that you should ask yourself in this process of identifying strengths as a part of a potential franchise could include the following when looking at the overall performance of an organization:

- What makes this franchise stand out among competitors?
- What, if anything, is most marketed and advertised by the franchise?
- What product or service is in highest demand, and likewise, how much profitability is accompanied by the sale of the given product or service?
- What has been the most profitable marketplace for the business up to this point?

In addition to performance by an organization, often identified by quantitative analysis, such as sales numbers, advertising costs, inventory turnover, quotas, net income, etc, there should also be a qualitative basis in understanding related to a franchise such as with leadership and experience found within the organization. To determine qualitative strengths that can be seen as a benchmark for success for a given franchise, try looking at answering questions such as:

- What leadership aspects within the organization have helped to motivate employees up to this point?
- What is the most positive attribute that other franchisees and leaders within the organization are mentioning when it comes to the franchise in question?
- What is helping the organization to stand out in customer service?
- What experience is added by existing team members and leaders within the organization that can be leveraged for additional success?

There are countless questions that a franchise candidate can ask themselves to help gain a better understanding of the true strengths that the franchise holds, but these should help to get you a good starting point- be sure to customize additional questions based on the specific industry or business model that you are considering. For example, for an individual looking to identify some of the strengths at Bio-One, I would probably want to know who the top performer has been and what do they attribute their success to. Every situation is different, but it is critical to identify the strengths of an organization before moving further in a SWOT analysis as strengths are the foundation of a company that allows for all other capabilities and development of resources that can be used to generate income and levels of competitive advantage in a competing industry.

Strengths of an organization, when looking inward from an analysis standpoint, can be found in both quantitative and qualitative information, such as the ability to create or deliver unique products or services, an organization's culture developed by leaders and team members, creating a unique atmosphere of top-notch customer service, sales and market share within a given marketplace, levels of training and development provided by franchisees, etc. Take these components and any additional that relate to the franchise in question to begin to develop an understanding of the driving factors and strengths that move the business forward. If it is hard to find strengths within a given franchise, then it should be pretty easy for you to move on to another option.

As a franchisee, you will want to be able to leverage strengths to overcome weaknesses; this is where we begin in looking at the analysis standpoint of an organization. We've taken a look at evaluating strengths within an organization, now let's take a look at the other end of the spectrum- Weaknesses.

Weaknesses

It's interesting, one of the factors that can be so detrimental to creating success within an organization is often the item rarely discussed, almost being a Taboo topic to discuss or bring up the possibility of having a weakness within the organization. I am a proponent of understanding the weaknesses within my organization, and myself as a leader, to be better prepared and work to overcome the obstacles ahead to be more successful moving forward.

An example that comes to mind when thinking about understanding weakness can be illustrated by looking at what a professional baseball player would consider to become a MVP-level athlete in Major League Baseball. A baseball player that is at the top of their game and career will continue to evaluate the areas for improvement that can be made in order to be the best possible athlete on the field in a given day, analyzing their batting statistics, base running percentages, fielding percentages, etc. to be able to see where additional fundamentals and technique may need to be analyzed and practiced further in order to achieve the goals set, such by winning the World Series or becoming the League MVP. If a baseball player went out onto the field everyday thinking that they were the "Best" and had no room for improvement, then they would soon be out hit, out ran, and out fielded by someone that was willing to put in the work to continue to become better.

I treat my business the same way that I would as a professional baseball player- I want to understand the areas where we may be performing in a weak manner or have room for improvement so that we can continue to leverage our strengths, overcome weakness, and maintain profitability and success. It is this same ideal that I feel necessary for franchisee candidates to consider-understand the weaknesses of an organization and determine if they are reasonably able to be overcome and quite possibly turn into additional strengths into the future.

Let's take a look at some of the questions you can ask yourself when reviewing the weaknesses of a potential franchise you are looking to invest in:

- What is causing the highest cost for the organization in question in business operations?
- What is the largest Overhead Cost associated with the franchise in question?
- What is the lowest performing sales category for products and services delivered by the franchise?
- What, if any, leadership channels or processes are hindering efficiencies within the organization?
- What attribute of the franchise is perceived most negatively by the market or public currently?

By putting the work in at the beginning of a SWOT analysis, specifically with analyzing Strengths within an organization, you will have a framework of asking additional questions based on understanding the weaknesses of the franchise in focus. In contrast to strengths, weaknesses of an organization can be understood as the inability for the business to effectively maximize available resources and processes to generate income or create a competitive edge in the industry. Identify strong and suitable questions to determine strengths of a franchise and use the same criteria, in opposite, to determine what the weaknesses of the franchise in question will be.

After identifying the weaknesses of a franchise, the next step will be to consider if the list of items that you have just uncovered can be overcome by the strengths that the organization has upheld. Here is a valuable set of "thinking equations" that may help you proceed further in the decision at this point:

- If Strengths are <u>Greater Than</u> Weaknesses = **Proceed Further with Analysis**
- If Strengths are <u>Less Than</u> Weaknesses = **Do Not Proceed Further with Analysis**

At this point, if you have determined that the franchise you are considering investing in as a franchisee, with time and assets, maintains strengths that will help to overcome any potential weaknesses found, or the strengths are considerably more powerful than weaknesses identified, then you should proceed to the next level of SWOT Analysis, Opportunities.

Opportunities

In evaluating strengths and weaknesses of a potential franchise, you have looked at what actual occurrences are currently happening at a given business. The factors of strengths and weaknesses can often be uncovered based on some sort of qualitative or quantitative approach, whether it be from a formula or an interview with an existing franchisee of the organization, but our next level of analysis can be considered somewhat of an "art form" when evaluating a franchise. Opportunities of a franchise, the next level of analysis for SWOT, are creating an understanding of processes in place by the business that will allow for additional improvement or sustainability into the future. The hard part of identifying opportunities of a franchise or other business model being analyzed is the fact that some opportunities can be easily anticipated or judged, whereas others may occur at random without any type of foreshadowing. Think of the internet boom in the 1990's as a good example of unperceived opportunities found with countless organizations throughout the world- the ability to market a product or service on the internet allowed "Mom and Pop Shops" to sell internationally and market across the globe to a whole new population of potential customers. This opportunity may have been unperceived by the organizations pre-internet, but the value was soon realized by many as soon as the boom took hold.

With the challenge in mind of being able to analyze opportunities, this gives you a little more freedom on the questions that you will inquire on in order to gain a knowledge-base of what can be achieved into the future based on the franchise in focus. Here are some examples that you can consider on your analysis of franchise options:

- Where do you see the product or service being delivered by the franchise move into the future?
- Are there additional, untapped, markets that you foresee as being possible profitability sectors for the franchise?
- Are there additional external factors that, if changed slightly or altered, could positively impact the performance of the organization?
- Is there something that, if made more efficient in current processing, could make the organization more profitable?

It is the "What If" questions that you want to be asking at this point in franchise analysis. The "What If" questions will carry forward the competitive edge that you will be working to create as a franchisee for the organization and can help create additional strengths that define competitive advantage in relation to the industry the franchise is competing within.

Threats

Similar to opportunities, threats have not yet occurred within a franchise that is under focus in your analysis process and may be somewhat more challenging to identify as compared to a weakness that is a clear underperforming category within the franchise. A threat, as identified as part of the SWOT Analysis, can be any external factor that can potentially harm a franchise's performance. From competing franchises within an industry to potential for market changes in a negative manner, threats can be vast. It could be easy, as a franchisee candidate, to get carried away in thinking about the potential threats that a franchise may face, and yes, it is important to gain an understanding for potential threats, but it is not healthy to become paranoid or overwhelmed by negative information that can often be easy to find with an internet search. To help make the process of identifying threats a little easier in your SWOT Analysis, here are a few questions to consider looking further into in relation to the franchise options you are looking to potentially invest in as a franchisee:

- What potential government regulations could alter the way of business currently for the franchise being considered and how likely is this to occur in the current political environment?
- What is the potential for new-competitor entry into the marketplace?

- What outside consumer groups or organizations have a negative outlook on the franchise or industry as a whole and what is the likelihood that they would disrupt business services?
- What vendors or outside support organizations are needed to maintain success within the business model and what potential factors could occur to sustain the business model?
- What sustainable leadership strategies are in place to help create sustainability in management and leadership functions in the event of high-level leaders leaving the organization for any reason?

After effectively answering each of the questions above, as well as any further that you have been able to create, you will have created a solid understanding of the four elements of SWOT Analysis. With the information that you have now developed and analyzed, you should have a better understanding of the franchise in question and will be able to begin to determine what strengths can be leveraged to overcome weaknesses identified and, likewise, what opportunities can help to potentially deter threats that have been considered. Having a solid understanding of the strengths, weaknesses, opportunities and threats of a franchise will make you a better leader in the organization that you chose to be a part of and the same understanding will help you to make the best decision as a franchisee candidate.

Marketing and Public Relations

In marketing, there is what is known as the 4 P's: Product, Place, Price and Promotion. As a potential franchisee, whether you have it realized it yet or not, you are getting ready to become a Marketing and Public Relations expert and will be fully engaged with each of the "P's." The ability to begin analyzing the aspects of product, price, place and promotion will be critical to maintaining success within the business model that you chose to pursue. By investing within a franchise, you gain access to a brand and logo and fundamental support to get running with marketing and promotions, but you must be able to continue these activities in a proactive manner in order to be successful for the sustainable future.

As the franchisee, you will be incorporating ideas of Fortune 500 companies with a much more defined and simplistic budget, but with the need to fulfill the same goal- attain more clients and match the services that you provide to a need that is set within the community or marketplace. Beyond community partnerships and having a sign above the door, there are additional aspects to the marketing spectrum that you will want to take into account, such as looking at developing Social Media campaigns, additional digital marketing, print advertising and more. Within a franchise, you are given the basics, but must be able to put the effort in to let the marketing channels help you to succeed.

Marketing techniques and ideas can be read about and learned through given scenarios, but the aspect of being comfortable in sharing a vision and being passionate about what you are sharing should be an inherent trait that is at the core of where you are sitting as a potential franchisee. In addition to the marketing channels and promotions you will be sharing, you will also be the public relations point of contact for your organization within the community, consistently helping to provide a positive outlook on your business model to individuals from an external standpoint. The perception of what others have on your franchise will greatly impact the ability to perform in a positive manner. This idea correlates directly to the focus at Bio-One where we help people first, then pursue business aspects. By leading a franchise with individuals at the forefront of your mind, and helping to fulfill an optimal need, positive reinforcement and perception of the organization will follow.

As a part of thinking and acting like a Fortune 500 company, if you are not yet comfortable with Marketing and Public Relations processes, it will be a good idea to look toward peer leaders within your community that you may be able to learn from, or even look into a marketing crash course with a local college or university. In addition to being the leader of the franchise, you will be the head marketing director and public relations manager.

Human Resources

If you are coming from the corporate world, you most likely are aware of the impacts of human resources on the daily integration of any process completed at your organization. It is the individuals within the business that make the wheels turn and the ones that help to provide a product or service to clients. As a franchisee, you will be the one that is going to help to hire, train and develop a team around you and will also be the one that will handle the human resource issues that may arise in a team atmosphere. It will be important for you to have a strong understanding of hiring and employment laws, especially if there are specific regulations required in the industry the franchise participates in, such as with Bio-One with hazardous materials where additional training or certifications may be required before a team member can work in a given scenario.

As the leader of the organization, you are at the helm of the franchise and will be able to develop a high performing team. Take the initiative to think about the skills and abilities you want to have as a part of your team and think about what success will look like when you begin to make those hiring decisions, also understanding that if the individual hired must be let go someday, you are also the one that will be telling them goodbye.

Working with Investors

To think like a Fortune 500 Company as a franchisee may start at the fundamental practice of taking on investors to help create the ability to succeed in the franchise model that you are looking to be a part of. Often times, the necessity to have some level of external investing will become necessary, either through SBA lending or private options as discussed in previous sections. The ability to work with the investing partners and platforms as a true partner will help to create additional success.

Fortune 500 companies that are publically traded on stock exchanges and maintain business structure from an international perspective also work with investors to help create success in a manner of sustainability. You may hear these investors as being called Shareholders, literally buying a portion of the company with the idea that it will succeed and pay dividends. The Shareholder places the hope and expectation on the corporation that the business model will maintain sustainable practices and will make positive decisions to make profitability a reality. Maintaining and developing this same idea as a part of being a franchisee is the next level of success when aligning your future franchise with the mindset of a Fortune 500 Company.

As a franchisee and business leader, envisioning your investors as Shareholders and Stakeholders will help you to make decisions as a part of the business model that creates sustainable success. Realizing that the decisions that you are making each and every day impact more than just your bottom line can help provide a business-centered compass to make decisions that will create additional success. This idea also correlates to balancing risk versus reward when analyzing potential strategies and decisions made for developing the potential for profitability.

Manage risk and make decisions that would make investors proud of being a part of your organization and you will build upon the successful traits being developed with your specific franchise.

Story of Success

> *If you are willing to do more than you are paid to do, eventually you will be paid to do more than you do.* – Anonymous

Your story is just beginning. You are working on making a decision that will impact the rest of your life, with the vision of success into the future. Throughout this book, you have received additional information that I hope will help to write your story of success and help to bridge the process of going from franchisee candidate to successful franchisee in a fast pace. As the Founder and CEO of Bio-One, we have helped to write success stories for many franchisees and in this next section I want to help give you a better perspective on the 100 Percent Success Model that we have developed and invite you to take a closer look as to how we can help you to write your next success story.

Bio-One and the 100 Percent Success Model

"Failure is not an option." Or "Nick does not let failure happen." Or "Failure is no longer in your vocabulary." – These are common phrases that you will hear many of my franchisees at Bio-One speak about because they are each true. As the owner, founder, and Chief Executive Officer of the Bio-One Franchise, I am proud to be able to say that we have a 100 percent success rate across all franchises that have been established to date. What is the fundamental reason behind this success? Not allowing others to fail.

Just coming across and saying something such as "I am not going to let you fail," sounds good on paper or in words, but is not truly beneficial unless there are positive and effective actions behind the model, or process, to create success. At Bio-One, there are several distinct characteristics of the franchise model that we have developed to ensure success: communication, priorities, and creating family.

Communication

From the beginning of a franchise relationship to the veteran stages, the ability to have clear and distinct communication is a fundamental priority to maintain success. By being able to claim a stake to 100 percent success model, the first recognition must be given to the fact that Bio-One has always promoted clear and fact-worthy communication across all relationships. Communication of expectations that I hold for franchisees are clear from day one and as the Chief Executive Officer of Bio-One, I consistently provide accurate information to potential franchisees in order for each to make the best decision that meets their personal goals and ambitions. If communication starts out as being non-trustworthy or broken, then a relationship will be broken thereafter resulting in negative performance.

Beginning with the end in mind, Bio-One emphasizes clear communication when franchisees are starting on their journey with the organization. This communication effectiveness is continued forward with training and resources provided for franchise locations to help provide a framework for a business model that has shown proven results for almost two decades. By providing support through available marketing resources and experience as well as fundamental training, franchisees hit the ground running at Bio-One without having to "reinvent the wheel" and can immediately begin focusing on acquiring clients and working to develop their priorities in business development based on the region involved. The priorities built upon by franchisees are the next key to having a 100 percent success model.

Priorities

Just as communication is a continual asset from every stage of becoming a franchisee at Bio-One, maintaining and developing priorities are also fundamentally critical to being able to preserve a 100 percent success model that few franchises throughout the world can hold acclaim to. Effective management and leadership of teams surrounding franchisees helps to make prioritization a simplified process and allows franchisees to maintain focus on the greater picture within their performance regions. As Chief Executive Officer, I continually emphasize the importance of developing priorities and action plans to meet given goals. If you, as a franchisee, were to come to me and say that by this time next year you want to make $1 Million, I will say that sounds like a top priority. But it goes much further than just stating that you have a priority or vision- Bio-One prioritization comes with action planning and development toward the goals established.

Prioritizing means that certain activities will be placed in higher importance and relativity as compared to other activities that may be put on hold or delegated to other team members, each of which align to the ability to achieve the end-goal set. Within priorities developed by franchisees, step-by-step action planning commences as a personalized roadmap to help achieve results and performance desired for each location; these action plans can include the goal for what relationships will be sought after within the community and what marketing or advertising strategies can be utilized to support the given mission. Additionally, prioritization within team development and client communication works hand-in-hand to further franchise performance. Building on one another, communication and prioritization would be minimal without the family atmosphere created at Bio-One.

Family Atmosphere

Some franchise models established throughout the world have been established with the purpose of turning through franchisees and locations as much as possible to yield returns based on fees of initiation and franchise buy-in. These franchise models don't look to their employees and franchisees as assets, but rather as another tool in the puzzle to adding funds in the pocket of the top tier of executives.

I am proud to say, as Chief Executive Officer and Founder of Bio-One, that you, as a potential franchisee, are the top asset that the organization can maintain right alongside the value of clients. Without people, there can be no business. Rather than creating competing interests between franchises, Bio-One has been developed in such a way that franchisees and leaders within the organization can rely on one another for support and feedback. There will be situations where advice from a veteran franchisee will be valuable to an incoming leader; likewise, there will be situations where the most recent franchisees provide a unique perspective or insight on a given situation and help to add value to a franchisee that has been with the organization for years. This reliability among peers at Bio-One helps to develop a family atmosphere that promotes positive results.

Success Breeds Success

❝Success seems to be connected with action. Successful people keep moving. They make mistakes, but they don't quit.❞ – Conrad Hilton

At Bio-One, we have developed an elite group of successful individuals that help to breed additional success as a part of the franchise. I feel that the best way to train and learn is by jumping in and experiencing it for yourself, but also being able to gain perspective and unique experience from those that have had success before you. As a part of the Bio-One success model, as the Chief Executive Officer, I have developed what I have come to call our "Success Team." Within the Success Team, we have combined multiple franchisees that have been with Bio-One from the beginning as well as several highly integrated attorneys that have built upon success from large franchise organizations, helping to bring unique perspective. In addition, the Success Team combines the experience and personal knowledge from our Chief Financial Officer who is also a Forensic CPA, who helps to build upon understandings from the ground up in the workings of franchises. As a Chief Executive Officer, it is my duty to surround the organization with individuals that help create success, and it is with this success team that we are able to individualize specialties at a macro-level and help to continually develop sustainable success. I will be the first to admit that I do not know everything when it comes to business and I help to drive this sustainability of success by engaging the Success Team and incorporating unique perspectives and vision as to where we can continue to be.

So, at the base of beginning to understand the inner-workings of the Bio-One franchise, the fundamental qualities of communication, priorities, family-orientation, and breeding success from success work alongside one another to create the platform for the 100 percent success model that many franchisees have already taken as an opportunity to make a dramatic change for the better in their lives and in the communities in which they operate.

Let's take a look at the testimonial by Todd Roach of Bio-One in Texas to help get a better understanding for how the family atmosphere has created success in his franchise.

Testimonial 3: Todd Roach, Bio-One

The next testimonial comes from another long term franchisee of Bio-One, Mr. Todd Roach, based in Dallas and San Antonio helps to illustrate a very honest perspective of what the life of a Bio-One Franchisee looks like. Within the following testimonial and interview recap, I feel that you can gain a personal outlook on the culture that we create to better the communities we are a part of and the clients that we interact with during some of the most challenging times that they may ever face.

Q: What kind of person does it take to be successful in the Bio-One Model?

A: The model isn't for everyone. I would say, first, you have to be very open for dynamic change. So, in what people would call the proverbial corporate lifestyle, things maintain a much steadier flow where you kind of know what you are doing when you go into work, you know how long your day is going to last and you kind of know and understand what your responsibilities will be- it doesn't usually differ out of those lines very much. With Bio-One it is quite a bit different- you have a framework of what you know is going to happen, but the business and the types of service requests that you get and the type of people that you interact with, and the vendors and employees that you manage will be very dynamic in nature in regards to the work that we do.

Since a lot of the work we get involved in has to do with tragic situations, we are not necessarily looking forward to when those things will happen nor do we know when they will occur, so the business flows with volatility within the workplace, if you will. And then, most people go to the stance of you "have to have a strong stomach to do what you do." That is true; this job is not for the faint of heart as we do see some interesting things. But once you get past that, really the biggest thing about this job is being a people person and being able to relate to the situation at hand. Again, it is not about getting in the door, making money, and getting out, it is really more about interacting with the client and trying to understand what has happened to them and where they are coming from and then how you can apply your skill and yourself to that project, basically to try and make their life better.

Whether the client lost someone or someone was hurt, or whether it be you are cleaning up something that has just gone long overdue, you are always walking into a situation where the client, whether they admit it or not, are looking for help from you. With this, you have to be very humble and you want to make sure that they get taken of and their emotional state and psychic state are considered as it varies up and down in every situation. One client, for example, could be extremely light hearted and easygoing whereas the next is completely opposite, so you have to be able to "go with the flow" of how you interact with each client.

It is not going in and just doing a job, it is going in and doing a job right. So that means there are certain protocols that you follow, certain steps that you always follow and regardless of how long a job takes or how tired you are, or how tired your crew is, the same steps and protocols need to be followed with each and every job. The "buck stops with me" in my organization, as it would with someone else who owned their own, and that is really one of the biggest things in making sure that you and your people both understand that this is the way in which we perform our jobs and we do our business and do it the same way each and every time. No shortcuts, no gray areas- always following it by the book and providing the best service that we can each and every time.

Q: Is this your first business after being a part of the corporate world?

A: Yes, it is my first business to own after being corporate. Prior to Bio-One is was in "Corporate America" IT, all of it, for a little over twenty years.

Q: How did you grow and expand so fast into two offices, San Antonio and Dallas?

A: With Dallas, I have grown up in the Dallas area for most of my life and I have a much stronger support base there in regard to resources that I know I can use, employees that I have, and people that I can call upon when I need them. It was much easier for me to set up a structure around the Dallas office in a way that it could be supported without me being physically there. I am still on the phone with Dallas every day, talking to the managers that are running the office and the vendors that we work with, but given the support structure that I was able to get in place relatively quickly, that afforded me the opportunity to not always have to be present.

Whenever I got to a point where I had a structure of people I could rely upon, we had made relationships with the vendors in which we wanted to use, and we had a pretty good structure of how the business was going to work week in and week out, that is when I decided I had the opportunity to come down to San Antonio and open up another office. At that point, Nick and I engaged and started talking about the opportunity to open the next office and things moved relatively quickly from there, allowing me to open the San Antonio office within the last month.

Q: Why do you think the Bio-One model is "Fail-Proof?"

A: There are a handful of reasons. First, Nick, as the owner and founder of Bio-One, has developed a community among franchisees in that we are not competitors to each other. If I need to pick up the phone and call a Bio-One owner in New York, I can, and I know the people there. If I need to call a Bio-One in Houston, I know I can, and know that the call will be answered and that the questions that I ask are going to be receptive to try and help. And vice versa, if they call me, I am willing to help them. This is really important, in that we have a really strong support structure where you may walk into a scene that you had not dealt with before or maybe you find yourself in a scenario where you need some guidance- so you have all of these different angles where you can reach out to for support.

Of course, we would always like to be able to reach out to Nick, given the fact that he started the organization, but I find myself more often taking the how-to questions and practices to the franchisee community; if there is anything strategic or business related or something that is financially impacting, that is when I will take the initiative to reach out to Nick and get his input. I would make sure that, one, he is ok with what I am looking to do from a brand-perspective and, two, get his input on the item I have a question on.

Number two, as a success factor with Bio-One, would be the business model that we try and drive home in comparison to competitors in that we are more worried about helping the client first then we are about being concerned about getting the money. That's really big. When I walk into a site, whether I am there to complete the job or submit a bid for the job, it has become common nature for me that I don't even bring up the payment part unless the client wants to. Sometimes clients are concerned that they have to pay for the services up front, which is not the case and I have even left jobs where the client was in a state of disarray given what was going on and it was not the appropriate time for them to figure out how to pay for the service or for me to approach them. In this case, I will complete the job and then revisit the client several days later to sort out the financial aspects and payments that will need to be completed. This is a strong element to the success within Bio-One, as money is not the only thing that is important to us, and I feel that this comes across when we are talking to them.

Additionally, we are very competitive with our prices; by and large we usually beat our competitors in the market, not necessarily from the standpoint of competitive bidding but just from what we initially come in with. Again, we are there to try and take care of the customer and not there for the best interest of "Todd," but first and foremost it is how we are going to help this customer and then figure out what is the best interest for Todd.

Then, the business itself caters to longevity because the service we provide will always be needed. It is not necessarily something that is "trendy" or will have a short lifespan. Our services are not like a new model of cell phone, there will not be a new option coming out in 6 weeks, so basically our services will be something that is needed for the long term. This is something that also caters to the success of the company, Bio-One.

Q: In your opinion, what are the 3 keys to success in the Bio-One model?

A: One, flexibility. Flexibility is not a broad enough word to encapsulate as to what I am trying to get at, but really you have to have flexibility with patience, flexibility with stress, and flexibility with resources. What that means is, in Corporate America, usually everything is laid out for you when you enter into a job place- you have certain people you work with, you have certain numbers you call, and you have resources you go to. As an example, if you are a software developer and you need new software, you go talk to your boss and you say, "Hey I need new software," and your boss buys it and gives it to you.

On the contrast, if you are in my line of work and you need something new or you need to figure out how to do something, a lot of times it is the First time; so you are making a lot of phone calls, you are trying to figure out what to do, you are hitting dead ends- so you have to be very patient and flexible in what you do. You are working with a lot of different people to try and coordinate one resolution to a job, so you really have to keep all of those pieces aligned in making sure that everything happens.

Number two- realize that we are 24/7. By and large, the majority of my calls do not come in after hours- a few do, but not nearly that many. However, you have to be open to the fact that your work life is now a part of your life, so a lot of people will say in Corporate America that you have your "Day Job" and then you have your "Life." Basically, when you are at work, you are working, and when you are at home, you are at home. With Bio-One, it becomes more a part of your personal life than a normal job would. You, again, have to be flexible in understanding about how you manage that. For some people that own a Bio-One organization that might not have a family or things of that nature, it is a little easier, but those of us that do have a family, you can spend all day working if you want to and you really just have to basically prepare yourself to know that, ok, I can figure out how to do these things in-between my life priorities.

Really the third thing is the human interaction part. There is probably really not a bigger piece of the organization that needs to be mastered beyond that, for all sorts of reasons. So again, the types of projects that we do are not glamorous- people do not like to talk about them- usually its things that we normally don't even like to think about, whether it is someone dying, taking their own life, someone being involved in a horrific accident, or something of that nature. These are the types of things that people don't like to talk about and people keep very close to themselves and, especially, when a third party shows up that they have never seen, it takes it one step higher.

So the people part of that is instrumental in that you have to be extremely confident as a business person to grow your business, but whenever you are approaching those client-situations, you need to be subtle and humble in your approach with that person. They, as the client, don't necessary care if you know how to do your job, they just lost somebody that was very close to them, and so you need to know how to manage that. On the flip side, if we are doing major hoarding remediation or things of that nature, that situation would be an emotional rollercoaster for the client, so you always have to be knowledgeable that, just because you walked into a project thinking that one game plan was going to take you to the end, it's likely that the game plan is most likely going to change two to four times during the course of a given project.

Most change is emotionally driven as there is a lot of talking and conversations with clients, so again, the people aspect is very important. If you think you are going to get into this business and you feel that you are going to be behind the scenes and just let it go do its thing, it is not going to work; you have to be willing to get out there and know what the people are going through, and you have to be willing to create a kinship with them so that you can understand what they are going through and be able to best resolve the issue that they are having.

Those would be the big three for me which would be the flexibility, ability to manage work with family, and then driving home the people aspect of it. The money will come. Obviously, the money is a very big part of it, and that will come as long as you focus on those big three, and I have had no issue with that myself.

Q: How long does it take to break even as a part of the Bio-One franchise?

A: I would say that anyone entering in fresh into a Bio-One market, they could look to break-even on their initial investment within 12 to 18 months. Some will be quicker; some will be slower, depending on the market that they are in. The volume will have a lot to do with the demographics and the population with where you work, so as an example, Dallas has about 11 Million People, Los Angeles has about 30 Million People, and so there is a 3 to 1 difference there. If I was running a Bio-One in Dallas and was also running a Bio-One in Los Angeles, and ran them the exact same way, data would tell me that I am going to clip my investment in Los Angeles, approximately three-times quicker than I would in Dallas. Now, my costs will also be higher in California as compared to Texas- people, the cost of resources, and how much is charged to clients will also be increased. Some of this difference will be "washed out" but there is a dramatic change in potential based on the population density differences. Depending on where you are, within a year to a little over a year, franchisees can look to clip their investment. Again, a lot of it goes back to how much the individual wants to invest them within the business.

There is not necessarily one "right way" but there are different ways to grow your business. You can be completely hands on and in it every day, 24/7, and that will move it along faster, or you can be a little more hands off and you can not be as "on it" and that will make the organization move a little slower. So, depending on what type of owner you want to be and where you want your company to end up and how fast you want it to get there, that is going to drive a lot as well.

Getting Your Business Up and Running Today

“The harder the conflict, the more glorious he triumph.” – Thomas Paine

Opening your own business may feel like the hardest thing you've ever done. However, you can relish in the fact that it will also provide the most glory once you've turned it into a successful enterprise.

The feeling of inspiration and having a wanting desire and drive to be successful is a great quality to possess. As a potential franchisee, you have demonstrated your passion for wanting to get a business up and running today and it is with this in mind that I would now like to invite you to take a closer look at the options you have considered in franchising and hope that you will consider Bio-One as an option if you feel this business model aligns with your interests and experiences. At Bio-One, we want to find a mutually beneficial relationship with a select group of franchisees and that is why we limit our expansion of franchise locations to no more than 12-15 per year. We want to welcome you as a potential franchisee and help to provide additional information that you may be inquiring about. To get started today with Bio-One, take a few moments to go to our website at BioOneInc.com and submit an interest form to get started along the process as you will be quickly contacted by one of our franchise coordinators that will help to guide you from step to step in creating success.

If Bio-One has helped to guide the way for perspective on enriching your life through becoming a franchisee, but you have decided to go another route that is more suitable to your strengths or passions, then time is still a critical component in this next stage. You have done the research and have worked to make the final decision as to where you will place your time, money and energy in the next chapter of your life, and it is the time period now that is most important to continue that action. Contact the franchise, directly, that you are hoping to be able to invest in and work to clarify their application process in order to start the ground work of developing success.

The process from first application or inquiry to having a franchise up and running can easily take a year for many franchises around the country, so the ability to get started on your individual process soon will be important to drive the engine of success forward. Take the highlights made available by this book and the insight shared by the franchisees of Bio-One and carry them with you in this next chapter of your life as a franchisee, and always aim to make a difference in not only your life, but the lives of others through positive and enriched business performance.

Bio-One and Creating Successful Franchisees

❝Success usually comes to those who are too busy to be looking for it.❞ – Henry David Thoreau

The 100 percent success model based in Bio-One has come from over two decades of hard work and perseverance toward several goals. In this final section, I would like to share the key points that have been discussed in detail and leave you with some last considerations to think about in creating successful franchisees and business leaders by the seemingly simplistic ideas that can be far-reaching, even more so beyond a career, and into the life that is carried at home and in the communities in which we serve.

Help First-Business Second

A successful franchisee will be developed with the mindset of helping people at the root of every service or product provided. By engaging the mindset that every action completed as a part of a business is to first help others within the community, and then have the potential to realize profitability, business leaders will have a more positive outlook on the activities performed as a apart of the organization and can help to inspire this same positivity in the lives and performance of others within the organization.

Success Breeds Success

By developing franchisees with focused and dedicated training, Bio-One emphasizes the importance of sharing success and enriching the lives of others through consistent investment in development. Always strive to learn something new every day and never lose sight of knowledge being the ultimate investment, and you will become a highly successful franchisee.

It Takes Hard Work

❝Character cannot be developed in ease and quiet. Only through experience of trial and suffering can the soul be strengthened, ambition inspired, and success achieved.❞ – Helen Keller

---

As a franchisee, you invest your money, your time and your energy into an idea that will hopefully become a success. At the foundation of this idea, you must be able to acknowledge and accept the reality that it is going to take an immense amount of hard work to succeed. What you put into "it" is what you will get out of "it." By placing hard work and effort into the franchise process as an incoming franchisee and continually being able to invest within yourself in gaining knowledge and experience, you will be able to develop a foundation for success that will continue for many years to come.

By placing a high level of effort and personal investment in the beginning, dividends will be paid for the long term as a part of a franchise. Never lose sight of the ones that also work hard for you day in and day out and continue to commit to their development and experience just as you do your own. By creating an empowered team that is working to better the lives of others, you will find success through any franchise model, and especially Bio-One.

At Bio-One, we will invest in your future by providing an incredible amount of training and experience that is unmatched. You will be given the opportunities to succeed and will be in an environment that is supportive and works to help the communities that we are a part of, always working to never re-victimize a client that has been a part of a traumatic situation that requires our services. If you are looking to be able to make a positive impact in your personal life as well as the lives of others, Bio-One just might be the place for you to start your career as a franchisee.

Welcome to the next chapter of your life, welcome to success.